{indulge}

{indulge}

Delicious Little Desserts That Keep Life Real Sweet

Kathy Wakile

with Miriam Harris

ST. MARTIN'S GRIFFIN NEW YORK

Food photographs by Andrei Jackamets
Food styling by Gig Aterio-Compton
Family photographs courtesy of the author
Photographs on pages 187, 191, 192, and 205 by Shutterstock

www.stmartins.com

Library of Congress Cataloging-in-Publication Data is available upon request.

ISBN 978-1-250-05126-4 (paper over board)

ISBN 978-1-4668-6444-3 (e-book)

St. Martin's Griffin books may be purchased for educational, business, or promotional use. For information on bulk purchases, please contact Macmillan Corporate and Premium Sales Department at 1-800-221-7945, extension 5442, or write specialmarkets@macmillan.com.

First Edition: September 2014

10 9 8 7 6 5 4 3 2 1

{ to the loves of my life }

Richard, Victoria, and Joseph—
you make each and every day so sweet.

{contents}

Introduction xiii

FALL

The Not-So-Forbidden Fruit

Fresh Fig Pizzette Bar 5

Pan-Roasted Fresh Figs with Infused Honey Syrup and Orange Mascarpone 7

Fresh Fig *Borsettini* 9

Figs in Baskets... 11

How Do You Like Them Apples!

Apple Crumblekins 16

Apple Ricotta Zeppolini 18

Petite Apple Pies 19

Caramel Apple Ravioli 23

Nuts for Nuts

Caramel Chocolate Walnut Tartlettini 28

Itty Bitty Pecan Pies...31

Pistachio-Apricot Mezzelune 33

Pignoli *Baklawa* Bites..37

Now That's Using Your *Googootz!*

Pumpkin Spice Babycakes..42

Pumpkin Spice Baby Bundts 44

Pumpkin Ginger Pecan Sticky Buns..45

Petite Pumpkin Pies with Toasted Marshmallow Topping 46

WINTER

For the Love of Cheesecake

Classic Cheesecake Cuties 54

Lemon Dream Cheesecake Cuties 56

Chocolate Cheesecake Cuties 58

Almond Joyous Cheesecake Cuties 61

PB&J All Grown Up

PB&J Wonder Cakewiches..66

PB&J Baby Bundts 68

Nutter Butter Finger Cakewiches 70

Hound Dogs...72

Chocolate—That's a Food Group, Right?

Chocolate Babycakes..76

Chocolate-Tangerine Baby Bundts...78

Chocolate Volcanoes 81

Nutty at Heart...82

Coffee and Cake

Blueberry Struesel Baby Bundts 85

SPRING

La Crema

Nonni Maria's Custard Cream 90

Zia Regina's Flan 92

Strawberry Panna Cotta 93

Chocolate Custard Tartlets 94

Choux Maker's Daughter

Pulcinelli Limoni 98

Strawberry Shortcake Puffs 100

Chocolate Hazelnut Kisses 101

Bananas Foster Cream Puff Cuties 102

Love Nests

Knafeh Nests 106

Doves' Nests 108

Blue Jays' Nests 109

Cardinals' Nests 110

. . . And *Who* Has More Fun?

White Chocolate Blondie Bites 113

Beach Baby Blondies 114

Bitsy Brunettes 116

Chocolate-Chili Brownie Bites 117

Mother's Day

Nonni Maria's Ricotta Wheat Easter Pies 120

Teta Melake's Lebanese Wheat Berry Pudding 122

SUMMER

Granita Splendida

Tony's Lemon Ice 131

Espresso with a Shot (or Not) 133

Pink Lady 134

Bottla Red 137

We All Scream for Gelato!

Strawberries-and-Cream 140

Orange Dreamsicle 142

Chocolate-Covered Cherry 144

Tanned and Salty 146

"Pick-Me-Up" (Italiano)

Tiramisu *Tradizionale* 151

Cioccolato Tiramisu 153

Capri Mia 155

Fuzzy Navel 157

Tutti Frutti BBQ

Grilled Plums with Basil–White Balsamic Syrup and
Lemony Crème Fraîche 162

Pineapple Kabobs with Coconut–Key Lime Cream
and Dulce de Leche Dunk 164

Grilled Banana S'mores 167

Grilled Cherry-Rosemary *Galettini* 170

BASICS

Basic Pastry—Single Crust 176

Basic Pastry—Double Crust/Lattice Top 177

Rustica Pastry 178

Simple Syrup 179

Orange Blossom Syrup 179

Caramel Drizzle 180

Ganache 181

Dark Chocolate Glaze 181

Raspberry Drizzle 182

White Chocolate Drizzle 182

Lemon Curd 183

Chantilly Cream 183

Chocolate Hazelnut Cream 184

Peanut Butter Buttercream 185

Marshmallow Cream 186

Acknowledgments 189

Index 195

Introduction

When reality TV came calling and I joined the cast of *The Real Housewives of New Jersey* I was already a housewife, *for real.* Stay-at-home mom, homemaker, wife, family COO—whatever the terminology—is a full-time, full-on occupation. It's my work, and I, like so many other women, take it very seriously. It's an important job—one I had no idea how deeply I could fall in love with when I first took it on. I have really and truly loved everything about it all these years, not least because, in being a wife and mother, I have found endless reasons to cook and bake and entertain pretty much nonstop. And I can honestly say I enjoy every minute—from our first Christmas Eve as newlyweds through all of our children Victoria's and Joseph's birthday parties to barbecues and every occasion in between. Both my husband, Rich, and I come from big families and we have a giant circle of friends, so our home is a hub of social activity, from small-scale impromptu visits to holiday feasts to the occasional all-night blowout.

I am a natural-born sweet tooth and, from the time I could wield a wooden spoon, an avid baker. I bake. *A lot.* Always have, always will. So when the cameras rolled in to my family's everyday life a whole lot of baking ended up on *The Real Housewives of New Jersey,* often in the middle of a whole lot of other, well, let's just call it "stuff" going on.

From day one I have been surprised and delighted by how many viewers related to me and my family and got in touch with me to compliment my desserts and ask for recipes. The response was so amazing and so touching! Sharing is at the very heart of what cooking is all about for me. It fulfills my desire to share with and care for others, from my nearest and dearest to the wider world. It must be something about the way my mother, Maria Pierri, was when I was growing up. The kitchen was always the place where you could find the largest gathering and where everything seemed to come together. So feeding my family and friends goodies I've made for them with love seems to be in my DNA. If you think about it, it really is one of the simplest ways to make another person happy, to let them know you are thinking of them.

I'm number four of five children. You all may know my baby sister, Rosie Pierri, who's such a strong presence on *Real Housewives of New Jersey*. What you may not know is that I have three older brothers, too: Ralph, Joe, and Anthony (they're a little camera shy). In addition to the seven of us in the immediate family, there was never any shortage of cousins by the dozens, aunts and uncles, *paisani*, neighborhood friends, school friends, girls my big brothers were dating, and so on. So, whenever my mother would bake, she did so for a small army. Naturally I inherited that instinct as well.

At the same time, making desserts is how I express my creativity, how I unleash my inner artist, and it's fulfilling on an individual level as well.

So I was very happy to share, but that didn't turn out to be so easy to do. At first, I replied to each request individually, with a thank-you note and a recap of ingredients and

(above) My uncle Domenico, Mom, me, and my Aunt Rosa harvesting tomatoes on the family farm in Italy. (right) Rosie, me, and Mom after my First Holy Communion.

(left) That's me cutting my birthday cake with Mom and Rosie looking on. I loved to entertain, even back then. (above) Here we are today.

prep instructions. The thing is, I cook pretty spontaneously and have never been big on writing things down—much like my mother and mother-in-law. It seems to be the Mediterranean family way; recipes are like folktales, the basic template is passed down and the details vary depending upon the mood, age, etc., of the teller. So that was a challenge. Plus, much to my amazement, the trickle of requests soon became a flood, which was incredibly gratifying but impossible to keep up with.

I think it was the Thanksgiving episode early on in my first season on the show that did it. I was at Melissa and Joe's, having happily volunteered to cover the desserts since she was doing the turkey and everything else. I did up a spread of all the desserts I always make for the holiday at my own home: teeny pies (apple, pecan, and pumpkin, of course),

little fig crostatas, dainty flutes of tiramisu (traditional, plus my *Capri Mia* and chocolate versions), some itty bitty brownie and blondie bites, and so on. And everybody flipped out—in a good way—from Joe and Melissa and all the guests to the crew and the producers. And the viewers! That's when it went from recipe requests to "Hey, Kathy: Where's the cookbook?"

Well, here it is!

I am so happy to share this collection of recipes, straight from my kitchen—a combination of Mediterranean desserts handed down from my mother (Victoria and Joseph call her Nonni) and other Italian relatives, and from my mother-in-law (whom the kids call Teta) and others on Rich's side of the family, which is Lebanese. Other recipes I have picked up from inspirations and experiences along the way (from frozen custard cones down the shore to candy bars at the sweetshop to *limoncello* in Capri) and more than a few I have made up on the fly—from experiments with fruit on the grill to improv moments. (One example of an improv moment was when I tested a new tartlet pan idea for presenting Zia Regina's flan last Thanksgiving. I couldn't seem to persuade the custards to come out of the pretty little pans, so there they sat alongside the dessert table. When my nieces Alexis and Malake noticed them, they asked, "Oh Aunt Kathy, can we have the crème brûlée?" My answer was, "Sure honey, enjoy!" Everyone was thrilled and raved about how it was the best crème brûlée they ever had. Did I mention that it was a mistake?

No? Oh, well, the secret is out now!)

The recipes are grouped by season, which is what guides me first and foremost as a cook—use what's in season at that time of the year and celebrate the traditions, ingredients, and cravings that go along with that season. I cook from the heart. I cook from memory. And I cook from spontaneous inspiration.

Within each season, you'll find several groupings of recipes. Each group is based on a central ingredient or theme and usually starts with something fairly basic and traditional—let's call it a base recipe—and then goes in all sorts of fun directions, i.e., apple crumble followed by apple zeppolini, then apple petite pies, then ultimately caramel apple ravioli.

For indulgence without sacrifice, all of my

(left) Here's the whole gang: Rosie and I are in front. (Do you LOVE my gloves?) Ralph, Joseph, and Anthony Jr. are in the back. (above) And, here's a picture of me ready for a Jersey Shore summer!

recipes are designed to yield individual-sized portions (in the ballpark of bite-size) in quantities large enough to share (usually at least one to three dozen). My philosophy is, "Go ahead—indulge. Have a cupcake. It's not gonna kill ya." The way I see it, if you have a little something that's packed with decadence, it delivers a lot of satisfaction in a smaller, more sumptuous package. And the more there is for the eye to savor, the better. It will taste even more delicious if it looks beautiful. Desserts are meant to make you feel happy. They don't have to be big to get that job done.

So the desserts in this book are all about being decadent and delicious and whenever possible, totally gorgeous. After all, we eat with our eyes first. You will find that some of my desserts are projects—that's how it is when you get creative. But there are plenty of tips on breaking things down into separate steps for making components ahead of time, and even some cheats and shortcuts if you aren't up for the full monty. (Plus some rescue remedies and straight-up camouflage for when things go awry—it happens to all of us!) These are the kinds of desserts where the process—from coaxing flour and butter into a lovely pastry dough, to stirring (and stirring and stirring!) cream and eggs in a double boiler until they thicken into a silky custard, to piping velvety swirls of frosting onto fudgy little cakes—is most definitely part of the pleasure. But, whether it's a simple homey treat like blondies or a sexy showstopper like chocolate volcano cakes, the very best part comes with the sharing of all that beauty and mind-blowing deliciousness. And that, my friends, is my reality.

Keep it sweet!
xoxo, Kathy

Me and Rosie, then and now.

{ fall }

It's always a bit of a shock when, once again, the school year begins, along comes a hint of a chill in the air, and pretty soon the leaves are blazing with color, blowing down from the trees, and piling up everywhere. Every year for as long as I can remember, whether trudging to school with my sister, Rosie, or picking my way through a pumpkin patch with Rich and the kids, I can hear and smell the holidays coming when I walk through drifts of fallen leaves, amid the rustling sounds and in the woodsy aroma of the drying foliage.

As I sadly kiss summer good-bye, I savor all the colors and smells and flavors of autumn and take great pleasure in the gradual transition from outside to indoors. I love how the season forms a bridge from days that are bright and breezy and still fairly long to times when darkness comes sooner, cold takes hold, and so do cozier cravings. By early October it has usually become chilly enough that I'm no longer all about avoiding using the oven. Quite the opposite: keeping the house warm and full of roasty-toasty smells is such a delight—a great consolation prize for losing the superlong days of summer when it stays light till eight or nine o'clock. No more pool parties and barbecues, but here come the holidays!

Aside from all of the traditional celebrations, fall is full of everyday joys like kids coming in from running around kicking leaf piles, with rosy cheeks and noses. I vividly remember being one of those kids and how good it was to come in to a nice baked treat, and I have loved doing the same with my own children.

This chapter focuses on four of my favorite key ingredients to cook with in the fall. Two of them are pretty obvious: apples and pumpkin (of course!). The other two are equally seasonal, but maybe more particular to my Mediterranean background: figs and nuts.

Fresh Fig Pizzette Bar

page {5}

The Not-So-Forbidden Fruit

Growing up back in the old neighborhood in Paterson, New Jersey, we had a fig tree in our backyard (we actually lived in three different houses and dug up and brought the tree with us each time we moved), and the annual fig harvest was one of the joys of late summer. The same was true (and still is) for many immigrants from the Mediterranean. Anyone with a patch of dirt grew a fig tree, and many of the trees were started from cuttings brought over from the Old Country—literally branches from the family tree back home, snipped off and carried in a pocket or baggage on the long boat trip to America. So it came to be that, half a world away from the Mediterranean, a treasured seasonal tradition has carried on for generations. Every year, just as summer began to fade, we loved to eat the figs as they ripened, straight off the tree and still warm from the sun.

Throughout the cold months, the tree was lovingly swaddled in burlap. I'm sure my American friends (as absurd as it may seem coming from a Jersey girl like me, everyone not Italian was referred to as "the American"—pronounced "Ameri-GAN") wondered what on earth it was, looking like a huge mummy sticking straight up out of the ground. I, of course, being young and American myself, thought everyone had a prized fig tree in their backyard.

My best beloved memory of those figs is from October of 1990, when Rich and I got engaged in the midst of the most gorgeous Indian summer Jersey ever had. He popped the question and presented me with a ring (in his parents' driveway—very gallant) on the fifth, which was a Friday. So that Sunday my parents had my future in-laws over for a celebratory meal, a traditional Italian Sunday lunch for about fourteen people—brothers, sisters, both sets of parents. Mom served up a beautiful feast: Sunday Sauce (yes, we call it sauce!), which is loaded with meatballs, sausage, braciole (yum!), plus antipasti, lasagna, veal Milanese, various *verdure* (veggies), and salad. It was such a happy occasion and of course everyone enjoyed the great meal Mom had prepared, but my parents and Rich's parents really didn't know one another yet, and there was a bit of a language and culture gap, since Rich's parents had come over from Lebanon when he was little, while my parents had both grown up in Italy. I'm sure both sets of parents were still trying to figure it all out.

But then, after dinner, my parents and my future in-laws walked outside to the backyard deck and my father presented them with a big basket of figs. The late heat had brought on the most bountiful harvest we'd ever had from our tree. This humble gift made such a connection between our families and our shared roots in the Mediterranean. Italians weren't the only ones bringing fig cuttings over from the motherland. Fig trees are growing all over America that started from branch tips carried over from Lebanon, Greece, Spain, Portugal, Turkey—all over the Mediterranean. Rich's mother and father's faces lit up. I could see it in their eyes: These people are like us.

Richie and I treasure this snapshot of our parents with the big basket of engagement celebration figs.

Fresh Fig Pizzette Bar

This is a great way to enjoy one of the most luscious crops of the fall season. The do-it-yourself element—everyone topping their own crust however they like—makes it fun for any casual gathering. You can go all out and have a big spread, with lots of different cheeses and nuts and syrupy toppings, plus a variety of figs if you are in an area where they are plentiful. But it's no less delightful if you keep it simple—a platter of sliced figs, a single spreadable cheese, a little dish of toasted chopped nuts, and a little jar of honey (or even jam). Either way, it's a lovely intermezzo (if you want to serve a more conventional dessert later) or dessert itself—a wonderful, relaxed way to end a meal and finish off the last of the wine.

·MAKES ABOUT 3 DOZEN·

CRUST

1 Rustica Pastry (page 178)

1 egg white (reserved from pastry), for brushing

Coarse sugar or cinnamon sugar, for dusting

TOPPINGS

2 dozen fresh figs, stemmed and sliced

Cheeses, such as Orange Mascarpone (page 7) to spread; creamy fresh ricotta or goat cheese; crumbled Gorgonzola or feta; thin slices of fontina; a wedge of softened Brie; shavings of Asiago; the possibilities are endless

Nuts, such as toasted and chopped walnuts, pistachios, hazelnuts, almonds, pecans

Infused Honey Syrup (page 7), Orange Blossom Syrup (page 179), (or whatever honey you like—light floral ones like orange blossom honey are especially nice with figs)

Preheat the oven to 350°F with two racks positioned in the upper and lower thirds of the oven. Line 2 large baking sheets with parchment paper.

On a smooth, lightly floured work surface roll out 1 disk of dough between 2 pieces of parchment paper to a thickness of between ⅛ and ¼ inch. Use a 3½-inch cutter to cut about 18 rounds, rerolling scraps as needed. Set the rounds on the prepared baking sheets, spacing the rounds about ½ inch apart, and use a fork to pierce each round all over. Repeat the process with the second disk of dough.

Beat the reserved egg white with 1 teaspoon water. Lightly brush the rounds with the egg wash and sprinkle with the sugar. (The rounds can be double-wrapped in plastic and frozen for up to 3 months. Thaw at room temperature before baking.)

Bake 10 to 15 minutes or until lightly browned.

If you are using cheese that's best served soft (such as Gorgonzola or Brie), set out 30 minutes before serving.

Arrange everything on platters and let everyone make their own pizzette—like a taco bar. Everyone takes a crust, spreads it with whatever cheese(s) they like, tops with nuts, figs, herbs, and a

Sprigs of tender-leaved fresh herbs, such as spearmint; basil (scented ones such as lemon, cinnamon, or pineapple basil would be great if you happen to grow them or know someone who does); fennel frond; marjoram.

equipment

3½-inch round cutter, or a glass, can, or bowl with an opening of that diameter

Two large baking sheets

drizzling of honey (that's the order that works best for the toppings to stay on, so it's a good idea to arrange your bar in that sequence).

shortcut: Use store-bought pizza dough, flatbread, or pita, brushed with butter and sprinkled with cinnamon sugar and baked.

note: The crusts are crisp, almost like tea biscuits, and they keep quite well. I keep them in a cookie jar or cracker tin and everyone in the house loves snacking on them. Some of my favorite ways to enjoy leftovers are to spread the crusts with whatever jam is on hand, or dip in milky tea, coffee, Nutella, etc. You can also opt to bake a half batch and freeze the remainder for other uses.

The crusts can also be cooked on a pizza stone on a medium-low grill.

Pan-Roasted Fresh Figs with Infused Honey Syrup and Orange Mascarpone

This sophisticated treat—on the savory end of the dessert spectrum—is popular with serious fig lovers. It's best served in very small dishes, like an amuse-bouche, and the toasted pistachios are essential to bringing the flavors and textures together.

MAKES 12 SMALL SERVINGS

ORANGE MASCARPONE

One 8-ounce tub mascarpone cheese, at room temperature

2 teaspoons finely grated Valencia orange zest (zested orange reserved to juice for Infused Honey Syrup)

INFUSED HONEY SYRUP

¾ cup honey

3 cinnamon sticks

2 star anise

2 cloves

2 teaspoons finely grated Valencia orange zest

¾ cup freshly squeezed orange juice from 2 to 3 good-quality Valencia oranges (one of them reserved from zesting)

1 dozen small fresh, firm but ripe figs, quartered

1 tablespoon unsalted butter

2 tablespoons Grand Marnier

½ cup unsalted pistachios, toasted and chopped

To make the orange mascarpone, drain any watery liquid from the top of the mascarpone, then put the cheese in a bowl, add the orange zest, and beat the mixture with an electric mixer on low speed just until creamy and light. (Can be made up to 2 days ahead and kept in an airtight container in the refrigerator.)

To infuse the honey, combine the honey, cinnamon sticks, star anise, and cloves in a medium, heavy-bottom saucepan and cook gently over medium-low heat for 15 to 20 minutes. Remove the saucepan from the heat and allow the honey to cool and infuse for at least 1 hour. (The infused honey can be made a few days ahead; remove spices and keep in an airtight container at room temperature.)

To make the honey syrup, use a slotted spoon to remove and discard the spices from the infused honey, then add the orange zest and juice to the saucepan. Bring the mixture to a simmer over medium heat, then lower the heat and continue simmering until the syrup is thickened and reduced to about ¾ cup, about 20 minutes. Take the pan off the heat and let the syrup cool to room temperature. (The honey syrup can be made a day ahead and kept in an airtight container at room temperature.)

To cook the figs, pour ¼ cup of the honey syrup onto a rimmed plate or small baking dish. Add the figs to the dish and turn to coat with the syrup. Melt the butter in a large nonstick skillet over medium heat. Cook the figs cut-sides down until golden brown, 1 to 2 minutes. Turn and cook 1 to 2 more minutes per side, or until the figs are tender and slightly softened. As the figs cook, they will release a lot of moisture that will quickly become a thick syrup; take care not to let them cook so long that they collapse and lose their shape. Use tongs to lift the cooked figs out of the skillet, leaving their syrupy liquid behind. Add the Grand Marnier to the skillet and cook 2 to 3 minutes, stirring often, to reduce by half. Pour the reduction into the reserved honey syrup and whisk to combine.

To serve, center a dollop (generous tablespoon) of orange mascarpone in each of 12 small serving dishes. Arrange a few fig quarters in each dish, drizzle lightly with the syrup, sprinkle with pistachios, and serve, with additional honey syrup in a small pitcher on the side (leftover figgy syrup keeps in the refrigerator for weeks— and it's delicious with vanilla ice cream or custard).

tip: Note that grating the zest of one orange should provide all the zest you'll need for both the mascarpone and the syrup, but it is nice to have additional zest for garnish. So use a zester to make long thin strips of zest from a second orange. Make sure you do your grating and zesting before you do any cutting or juicing (if you haven't already made this mistake, trust me, you do not want the hassle of trying to get the zest of any citrus fruit that isn't whole and unsqueezed). And make sure you take off only the thin, colored layer of peel—none of the bitter white pith. You'll need 2 to 3 good-quality Valencia juicing oranges for zest and juice.

Fresh Fig Borsettini

Borsettini is Italian for purse and is often used in names for filled pastas. I think the purse reference is to the money pouches from centuries past, because the pastas look like little bags that have been cinched at the top. Here, we have pastries that look more like elegant little clutches and—packed with aromatically spiced figs, drizzled with dark, figgy syrup, and sprinkled with toasted pistachios—taste amazing.

FIG FILLING

1 cup packed dark brown sugar

1 teaspoon cinnamon

½ teaspoon freshly grated nutmeg

½ teaspoon cardamom

Pinch fine sea salt

2 dozen small fresh figs, stemmed and quartered

4 tablespoons (½ stick) unsalted butter

½ cup fresh orange juice, plus more as needed

CHEESE FILLING

8 ounces chèvre, softened

¼ cup heavy cream

½ teaspoon finely grated lemon zest

Pinch fine sea salt

2 tablespoons honey, optional

1 large egg yolk (white reserved for brushing dough)

1 teaspoon vanilla extract

PASTRY

1 recipe Basic Pastry Single Crust (page 176)

To make the fig filling, combine the sugar, cinnamon, nutmeg, cardamom, and salt in a large mixing bowl and stir with a fork to mix thoroughly. Add the figs to the bowl and mix to coat.

Melt the butter in a large heavy skillet over medium heat, tilting the skillet to distribute the butter evenly. Add the figs to the skillet, using a spoon or flexible rubber spatula to scrape all of the sugar-and-spice mixture off the sides of the bowl and into the skillet. Add the orange juice and stir gently. Bring to a simmer over medium heat and cook the figs, stirring occasionally, for about 20 minutes, or until the liquid is very thick and gooey. Be sure to stir more frequently toward the end of the cooking time when the liquid is becoming thick enough to stick to the skillet and scorch. Turn off the heat under the pan and leave the figs to cool to room temperature. (The figs can be made ahead and kept in an airtight container in the refrigerator for up to 2 days.)

To make the cheese filling, combine the chèvre, cream, lemon zest, salt, honey, egg yolk, and vanilla in a mixing bowl and beat with an electric mixer until creamy, 1 to 2 minutes. (The cheese filling can be made up to 2 days ahead and kept in an airtight container in the refrigerator.)

To prepare the dough, lightly dust a smooth countertop with flour and roll each disk of the dough out to an even thickness of about ⅛ inch (not too thin, or it will become difficult to handle and fall apart). Tightly wrap each sheet of dough with plastic and return to the refrigerator for 15 minutes or until you are ready to cut

1 large egg white, for brushing

¼ cup coarse raw sugar, for sprinkling

½ cup pistachios, pecans, or walnuts, toasted and chopped, for serving

equipment

4-inch round cutter with plain or scalloped edges, or a glass, can, or bowl with an opening of that diameter

Two large baking sheets

the dough into rounds for the pastries. (Dough can be kept in the refrigerator overnight or double-wrapped and frozen at this stage for up to 3 months. Defrost for 1 hour before using.)

Preheat the oven to 375°F with two racks positioned in the upper and lower thirds of the oven. Line 2 large baking sheets with parchment paper.

Use a 4-inch cutter to cut each sheet of the chilled dough into about a dozen rounds, rerolling any scraps. (The cut rounds can be tightly wrapped and refrigerated overnight or double-wrapped and frozen for 1 month.)

Divide the dough rounds between the two parchment-lined baking sheets. Onto the bottom half of each round drop 1 scant teaspoonful of cheese filling and top with 2 fig quarters, using a fork to lift the figs out of their gooey syrup and reserving the syrup (for serving). Fold the top half of the dough over and seal the edge by pressing gently with a fork. Use the tip of a small sharp knife to make a teeny X in the top of each pouch.

Beat the egg white with 1 tablespoon water. Lightly brush the pastries with egg wash and sprinkle with coarse sugar. (Can be frozen on baking sheets, then transferred to freezer bags and kept frozen for up to 1 month. Bake without defrosting, adding about 5 minutes to the baking time.)

Bake the pastries until lightly browned, about 15 minutes, rotating halfway through the baking time. Let cool 5 minutes before serving, or serve at room temperature.

To serve, gently rewarm the reserved fig syrup in a small saucepan (or in a heatproof bowl on low heat in the microwave), whisking in orange juice 1 tablespoon at a time to reach a pourable consistency. Lightly drizzle the borsettini with syrup and sprinkle with toasted nuts before serving.

shortcut: Use premade pastry dough.

Figs in Baskets

I created these using a very specific type of baking pan: Chicago Metallic Lift & Serve Single Squares Pans. I don't know of any pans that give the same size and shape, which are totally perfect for this treat, providing just the right ratio of pastry to filling. Figs are earthy, rich, and dense—overly so if the balance isn't right. At the same time, you don't want too much crust, either. These little goodies have just the right amount of each. A perfect two-bite treat—great with coffee.

FIGS

1 cup soft dried figs, stemmed and coarsely chopped

⅔ cup water

½ cup fresh orange juice

¼ cup packed light brown sugar

4 tablespoons (½ stick) unsalted butter, melted and cooled

2 large eggs, lightly beaten

1 teaspoon vanilla extract

¾ cup coarsely chopped walnuts, optional

BASKETS

1 recipe Rustica Pastry (page 178)

1 egg white (reserved from making pastry), for brushing

Coarse sugar, for dusting

equipment

3½-inch round cutter or a glass, can, or bowl with an opening of that diameter

Two 12-cavity Chicago Metallic Lift & Serve Single Squares pans

Food processor

Pastry tamper, optional (very handy—especially if you have Jersey nails!)

To make the filling, combine the figs, orange juice, sugar, and ⅔ cup water in a medium heavy-bottom saucepan and simmer over low heat, stirring occasionally, until the figs soften, 10 to 15 minutes. Let the mixture cool slightly, then pour it into the bowl of a food processor and pulse just until finely chopped (do not purée). (At this point, the fig mixture can be transferred to an airtight container and refrigerated overnight. Bring to room temperature before continuing with the recipe.) Transfer the mixture to a large bowl and stir in the butter, eggs, vanilla, and walnuts. Mix well.

Preheat the oven to 350°F with a rack positioned in the center. Lightly coat the baking pans with nonstick cooking spray or vegetable oil from an oil mister.

To form the pastry baskets, on a smooth, lightly floured work surface roll out 1 disk of dough between 2 pieces of parchment paper to a thickness of ⅛ inch. Use a 3½-inch cutter to cut 12 rounds, rerolling scraps as needed to make all 12 rounds. Carefully transfer each round to the baking pan, using a pastry tamper or your fingertips to neatly mold each circle into the pan. Use scissors or a small sharp knife to cut away any excess dough. If the dough tears when you are fitting it into the pan, no worries. You can easily patch it back together; it will hold and not show. (Gather up the dough scraps, pat together, wrap tightly, and reserve in the refrigerator; you will use it for the basket weave tops.) Repeat the process to make 12 more rounds, gathering up the dough scraps and adding to the packet of reserved dough in the refrigerator. Transfer

the pans to the refrigerator to keep the dough cool while you roll and cut the strips for the basket weave tops.

To cut the dough for the basket weave tops, roll out the reserved trimmings into a large rectangle about 6 inches across and about 12 inches long, with an even thickness of ⅛ inch. Then use a knife, pastry cutter, or pizza wheel (and a ruler or straight edge if you like) to cut the rectangle in half crosswise and into thirds lengthwise. This will give you 6 rectangles of dough. Cut each rectangle crosswise into 16 strips each, about ¼ inch wide and 4 inches long.

Scoop about ¼ cup of fig filling into the chilled pastry shells (I like to use a mini scoop to keep things neat).

To weave the lattice tops, lay 2 strips parallel across each tartlet, spacing evenly. Lay a third pastry strip across the middle of the tartlet, perpendicular to the first strips. Weave it over and under the first two strips, then add a fourth strip and weave it in the opposite direction. Fold back the rim of the shell over the edge of the lattice strips and crimp to secure.

Whisk together the egg white and 1 tablespoon water. Lightly brush the egg wash onto the tops of the pastries. Sprinkle with coarse sugar and bake 10 to 15 minutes, or until the edges begin to turn light golden brown and the fig filling is bubbly. Rotate the pans halfway through baking time.

Set the pans on wire racks and cool to room temperature. Use a small spatula or a fork to carefully ease the pies out of the pans. Serve at room temperature.

> *shortcut*: Use store-bought puff pastry, premade pie dough, or shallow premade pastry shells.

*Apple
Crumblekins*

p a g e {**16**}

How Do You Like Them Apples!

Apples. So all-American. So wholesome. So plentiful and varied. So underappreciated! Maybe it's because apples are one of the first fruits we eat as kids and they become a fixture in our diets early on, but it seems to me that apples end up being taken for granted, and apple desserts are often thought of as nothing particularly special.

But apple desserts can so easily be made very special. I could write a whole book of apple treats, but here I've put together four of my family's top favorites. First come the crumblekins—so perfectly delicious and so easy you can throw them together in the middle of making dinner most any evening or otherwise multitasking, as we all seem to do way too much these days. In my first season as one of *The Real Housewives of New Jersey*, I was making apple crumblekins in one of my many kitchen scenes and I have received so many requests for the recipe. So here you go—"Sharing is caring." Then there's the zeppolini—aka fritters—to die for. Put in a bit more (but not a whole lot more) time and effort, and you can make a simple piecrust, cut it to fit muffin pans, load them up with the same filling as for the crumblekins, and you have darling apple pies. Last up is my tribute to one of the great joys of childhood, the caramel apple—in the form of a pastry pocket that I'm calling a "ravioli" filled with apple and drizzled with caramel.

Apple Crumblekins

Putting the ultimate homespun dessert in little individual ramekins brings the humble crumble a little elegance (it doesn't get shoveled out of a big casserole dish and piled on the plate). I like to overfill the ramekins ever so slightly so that just a little of the sugary-appley-cinnamony juices bubble down the sides (I line the baking sheets with parchment so I don't have to scrub them). If you leave a bit too much room—because you didn't have quite as many apples as you thought, you're stretching the recipe to make more servings, or you're experimenting with baking dishes of different dimensions than called for—don't despair. Top the crumblekin with a scoop of your favorite ice cream or gelato! Vanilla always works but maple walnut, caramel butter pecan, and rum raisin are fine choices, too. If ice cream isn't your thing, Chantilly Cream (page 183) is also great.

• MAKES ABOUT 1 DOZEN •

APPLE FILLING

4 medium crisp, tart apples

½ lemon

¾ cup packed light brown sugar

1 tablespoon all-purpose flour

¾ teaspoon cinnamon

¼ teaspoon nutmeg

¼ teaspoon fine sea salt

2 tablespoons cold unsalted butter, cut into 12 pieces, for dotting tops of crumbles

CRUMBLE TOPPING

½ cup all-purpose flour

½ cup rolled oats

½ cup packed light brown sugar

6 tablespoons cold unsalted butter, cut into small cubes

1 teaspoon cinnamon

½ cup chopped walnuts

½ cup raisins or sweetened dried cranberries

Preheat the oven to 350°F with a rack positioned in the center. Generously grease the ramekins.

To make the filling, peel, core, and chop the apples into ¼ to ½ inch pieces and transfer them to a large mixing bowl (you should have about 6 cups of chopped apples). Squeeze the lemon over the top and toss lightly to combine. Add the sugar, flour, cinnamon, nutmeg, and salt to the apples and mix thoroughly. (At this point the apple filling can be stored overnight in an airtight container in the refrigerator.)

To make the crumble topping, combine the flour, oats, sugar, butter, and cinnamon in a large mixing bowl. Blend with your fingers until the mixture resembles coarse crumbs. Add the nuts and raisins and mix lightly with your fingers to incorporate.

Spoon a few tablespoons of apple filling into each ramekin, filling about ¾ of the way up to the rim and packing firmly with the back of the spoon. Top the filling with a piece of butter, then spoon on a heaping tablespoon of topping and pat gently to settle it down onto the apples, mounding up the topping a bit as the apples will shrink as they cook.

Set the ramekins on a rimmed baking sheet. (This will make the ramekins easier to handle and catch any drippings that bubble over during baking; or go a step further and line the sheet with foil or parchment paper to make for really easy cleanup.) Bake on the middle rack for 20 to 30 minutes, or until nicely browned and bubbling, rotating the tray midway through the baking time. Let cool 10 minutes before serving.

> tip: In a pinch, you could use a muffin pan with foil cup liners or doubled paper liners instead of the ramekins. It makes for a less charming presentation, but it works.

Apple Ricotta Zeppolini

These knobbly little pillows of apple deliciousness are not impressive to look at. I think of them as the Cabbage Patch dolls of my dessert repertoire—so ugly they're incredibly cute. But here's what you need to know: Whatever these easy-to-make treats may lack in elegant looks, they more than make up for in flavor—*delicioso!* A huge hit with eaters of all ages.

• MAKES ABOUT 3 DOZEN •

1 cup all-purpose flour

2 teaspoons baking powder

4 tablespoons (½ stick) unsalted butter

¼ teaspoon fine sea salt

¼ cup granulated sugar

1 cup whole-milk ricotta

1½ teaspoons vanilla extract

3 large eggs

1 large crisp apple, peeled and grated

1 teaspoon lemon zest

4 to 6 cups canola or vegetable oil, for frying

CINNAMON SUGAR

½ cup granulated sugar

1 generous tablespoon cinnamon

Sift together the flour and baking powder into a large mixing bowl; set aside.

In a medium saucepan combine the butter, salt, sugar, and ricotta. Mix gently over low heat and warm thoroughly.

Take the saucepan off the heat and stir in the vanilla and the flour mixture, stirring continuously until a ball is formed.

Transfer the mixture back to the large mixing bowl and with an electric mixer or by hand beat in the eggs one at a time, making sure each egg is incorporated before adding the next. Beat until smooth. Add the grated apple and lemon zest and stir to combine.

Pour the oil into a large, deep, heavy-bottom skillet or pot. Heat over medium heat to bring the oil to 325°F on an instant-read thermometer.

Working in batches (this is important: crowding will lower oil temperature and cause the zeppolini to absorb too much oil), use two small spoons to carefully drop teaspoon-size blobs of zeppolini dough into the oil. The zeppolini will float to the top as they cook. Cook, turning once or twice, until puffed and evenly golden brown all over, 4 to 5 minutes total.

Remove zeppolini with a slotted spoon and drain on paper towels.

Whisk together the sugar and cinnamon. Toss the warm zeppolini in the cinnamon sugar and serve, still warm.

> In the unlikely event of leftovers reheat in a 350°F oven to recrisp.

Petite Apple Pies

What could be more classic, more delightful than a freshly baked, homemade, lattice-top apple pie? Little individual ones that everyone gets to enjoy all to themselves! Be sure to grease the pans generously so the little pies pop out with their golden brown pastry crust intact. And set the muffin pans on a baking sheet before baking; this makes it easier to get the pies in and out of the oven without dinging the lovely crimped edges.

• MAKES 1 DOZEN •

Basic Pastry—Double Crust/ Lattice Top (page 177)

FILLING
1 recipe Apple Filling from Apple Crumblekins (page 16), butter omitted

1 egg white, for brushing

2 tablespoons coarse sugar

equipment

Heavyweight nonstick 12-cavity standard-size muffin pan

4½-inch round cutter, or a glass, can, or bowl with an opening of that diameter

Pastry tamper, optional

Generously grease the muffin cups with butter.

Prepare the pastry dough as instructed. Divide into thirds, wrap tightly, and chill thoroughly.

Prepare the apple filling as directed in the Apple Crumblekins recipe, omitting the butter.

On a smooth, lightly floured work surface, roll out 1 of the chilled disks of dough to an even thickness of about ⅛ inch. Use a 4½-inch cutter to cut out 6 circles of dough. (The dough circles can be layered with parchment or wax paper, wrapped tightly in plastic, and refrigerated for up to 2 days; or double-wrapped and frozen for up to 1 month.)

Carefully transfer the dough circles to the muffin pan, pressing gently with a pastry tamper or your fingers to mold the dough to the cup (it should overlap the edge of the cup by at least ¼ inch). Gather up the dough trimmings, wrap tightly, and set in the freezer to chill. Roll out the second disk of dough and cut it into 6 rounds, adding the trimmings to the reserved dough in the freezer. Fit the dough rounds into the remaining 6 cups in the muffin pan.

Transfer the muffin pan to the refrigerator.

Preheat the oven to 425°F with a rack positioned in the center.

To cut the dough for the lattice tops, add the reserved dough from the freezer to the third disk of dough, then divide in half. Put

one half back in the refrigerator and roll the other half out into a rectangle about 6 inches across and about 12 inches long, using the flat edge of a large knife to straighten the edges as you roll the rectangle to an even thickness of ⅛ inch. Then use the knife, a pastry cutter, or a pizza wheel (and a ruler or straight edge if you like), to cut the rectangle crosswise into 24 strips. Repeat the process to roll and cut the other half of the dough into 24 more strips.

Fill the chilled pastry shells generously with apple filling. Use a spoon to mound the filling and pack it down fairly firmly in each muffin cup, as it will sink a little when it bakes.

To weave the lattice tops, lay 2 strips parallel across each tartlet, spacing evenly. Lay a third pastry strip across the middle of the tartlet, perpendicular to the first strips. Weave it over and under the first two strips, then add a fourth strip and weave it in the opposite direction. Fold back the rim of the shell over the edge of the lattice strips and crimp to secure.

Whisk the egg white with 1 tablespoon water. Lightly brush the pastry lattices with the egg wash, then sprinkle with the coarse sugar.

Set the muffin pan on a rimmed baking sheet and bake at 425°F for 15 minutes, then rotate the baking sheet, lower the temperature to 350°F and bake for another 15 minutes, until the filling is tender and bubbly and the pastry crust is nicely browned.

Set the tray on a wire rack and let the pies cool in the pan for about 10 minutes. Use a small spatula or a fork to carefully lift the pies out of the pan and transfer to a wire rack to cool to room temperature before serving. Best made at least 1 day ahead. Store at room temperature covered in foil (not in an airtight container, and don't cover until completely cooled, as this will make the crust soggy).

shortcut: Use premade pastry dough.

Caramel Apple Ravioli

Ravioli is one of the best-loved items in traditional Italian cooking. What's not to love? Especially when you're treated to homemade ones—tender dough pockets with tasty filling. They're dumplings, for crying out loud! Yum! For my sweet spin on ravioli, I brought the all-American and superautumnal flavors of caramel apple into the mix. Fair warning: These take some time to make, but they are so worth it. I created them early on in the process of developing the idea for this book, and my family went bonkers for them. Joseph, who's my all-American boy when it comes to desserts, insisted these were "keepers" for the book—can't say no to that! Then I brought a batch with me when I went to meet my prospective publishers in New York City—knocked their socks off. (Seriously, I think these little delectables helped me land a book deal! Never underestimate the power of pastry, my friends.) So, yeah, they are a little labor intensive; I make the most of my efforts by making them in bulk—this recipe doubles (and triples!) really well, and the whole unbaked pastries can easily be frozen, so I always make extra to pop into the oven anytime.

⸱ MAKES 20 ⸱

PASTRY

2½ cups all-purpose flour

1 teaspoon fine sea salt

½ teaspoon freshly grated nutmeg

½ teaspoon cardamom

8 ounces (2 sticks) unsalted butter, cold, cut into ½-inch cubes

⅓ cup ice water, plus more as needed

APPLE FILLING

2 medium crisp apples (about 1 pound)

2 teaspoons freshly squeezed lemon juice

½ teaspoon cinnamon

⅛ teaspoon nutmeg

To make the pastry dough, combine the flour, salt, nutmeg, and cardamom in the bowl of a food processor fitted with the standard blade. Pulse to mix, then add the butter and pulse a few more times, just until the mixture resembles very coarse cornmeal. Add ⅓ cup ice water, then pulse the machine a few more times. Add more water, 1 tablespoon at a time, pulsing only enough to uniformly combine the ingredients—just until the mixture begins to gather together, but not long enough to allow it to form a ball.

Turn the dough out onto a large sheet of wax paper. Lightly press the pieces together through the paper. Then divide the dough in half and lightly pat each half into a rectangle about ¾ inch thick, wrap tightly in the wax paper, and refrigerate until well chilled, at least 1 hour.

To make the apple filling, peel, core, and finely dice the apples, transferring them to a large mixing bowl. Add the lemon juice, tossing to coat. Add the cinnamon, nutmeg, flour, and salt and mix well to combine.

(Recipe continued on next page)

1 tablespoon all-purpose flour

Pinch fine sea salt

2 tablespoons unsalted butter

¼ cup packed light brown sugar

CHEESE FILLING

4 ounces cream cheese, softened

2 tablespoons confectioners' sugar

2 tablespoons whole-milk ricotta cheese

1 teaspoon finely grated lemon zest

Pinch fine sea salt

1 large egg yolk (white reserved for brushing dough)

½ teaspoon vanilla extract

¼ cup walnuts or pecans, lightly toasted and finely chopped, optional

1 large egg white, for brushing

Coarse raw sugar, for sprinkling

Caramel Drizzle (page 180), for serving

Toasted chopped walnuts or pecans for serving, optional

equipment

Food processor

Electric mixer

Large rimmed baking sheets

Melt the butter in a large skillet over medium-low heat. Stir in the brown sugar until melted, then add the apple mixture to the pan, raise the heat to medium, and simmer, stirring occasionally, until the apples are tender and the liquid in the skillet has evaporated, 5 to 10 minutes. Set aside to cool to room temperature. (The apple filling can be made a day ahead and kept in an airtight container in the refrigerator.)

To make the cheese filling, combine the cream cheese, confectioners' sugar, ricotta, lemon zest, and salt in a large mixing bowl and beat with an electric mixer until light and fluffy. Add the egg yolk and vanilla and beat to incorporate. Stir in the nuts. (The cheese filling can be made a day ahead and kept in an airtight container in the refrigerator.)

Preheat the oven to 375°F with a rack positioned in the center. Line 2 large baking sheets with parchment paper.

Lightly dust a smooth work surface with flour and roll out one portion of the dough as a 10 by 15-inch rectangle, with an even thickness of ⅛ to ¼ inch (not too thin or it will become difficult to handle and fall apart).

Use a pastry cutter or sharp knife to cut the dough lengthwise into 2½-inch-wide strips. Then cut each strip crosswise into 2½-inch squares. (You should end up with 20 squares.)

Arrange the first set of pastry squares on the parchment-lined baking sheets, spacing them about 1 inch apart. Spoon 1 scant teaspoon of cheese filling onto each square. Use the back of the spoon to spread the filling in an even layer, leaving a ½-inch border around the edge. Top the cheese with about 1 teaspoon of apple filling.

Roll out and cut the remaining rectangle of dough into 2½-by 2½-inch squares. (You should end up with another 20 squares, to top the filled ones.)

Lightly beat the egg white with 1 tablespoon water. Use a small brush to lightly coat the edges of the filled dough squares with egg wash. Lay a square of dough over the top of each and gently press the edges together with a fork to seal. Carefully use the tip of a very sharp paring knife to make a tiny, X-shaped vent in the top of each pouch (this will allow steam to release during baking).

Lightly brush the tops and edges of the little pouches with the remaining egg wash, then sprinkle the ravioli with coarse sugar. (The pastries can be frozen at this stage for up to 3 months. Freeze on the baking sheets, then transfer to heavyweight plastic freezer bags. Don't thaw before baking; just add a few minutes to the baking time.)

Bake 25 to 30 minutes, or until tops and edges are golden brown, rotating the sheets halfway through the baking time.

Let cool 1 to 2 minutes, then carefully transfer the ravioli to a wire rack. Serve slightly warm, drizzled with caramel and sprinkled with toasted nuts.

Caramel
Chocolate
Walnut Tartlettini

page {28}

Nuts for Nuts

G rowing up, throughout every autumn there was a big bowl of whole, shell-on nuts on the kitchen table—most often walnuts, almonds, pecans, or hazelnuts. There were a couple of nutcrackers tucked in the bowl, and we'd crack open a few nuts to munch on whenever we wanted a snack (there was never, ever any packaged snack foods in the house). My Lebanese in-laws are the same, and it's common in many Mediterranean households.

Nuts remain one of my favorite foods—on their own, in savory dishes, and most especially in desserts, where each type of nut brings a buttery earthy decadence all its own. Nuts are such a simple, smart food, with such great substance and crunch and texture. Plus they're good for you! All right, all right, enough of all that . . . I love nuts, so they have an important place in my book! I hope you like them, too. *Buon appetito!*

Caramel Chocolate Walnut Tartlettini

The pastry for these teensy tartlets is really just a very thin lining for the mini muffin cups; it will warm up as you work with it and might become a little slippery and prone to tearing—if so, just park the whole pan in the fridge for a few minutes and let the dough firm back up. You can do this several times if need be; the little tarts will still bake up just fine. Also, the dough doesn't need to come all the way to the rim of each cup, just don't overfill when you put the filling in. When the tartlettini bake, the shell and the filling meld together beautifully into a swoony little confection that I've been told is like what would happen if a chocolate chip cookie and a walnut brownie had a baby—and drizzled it with caramel. You're welcome!

•MAKES ABOUT 3 DOZEN•

CHOCOLATE PASTRY

4 ounces cream cheese, at room temperature

8 tablespoons (1 stick) unsalted butter, at room temperature

1 cup all-purpose flour

3 tablespoons cocoa powder

¼ cup confectioners' sugar

¼ teaspoon fine sea salt

CHOCOLATE WALNUT FILLING

1 cup packed light brown sugar

4 tablespoons (½ stick) unsalted butter, melted and cooled

1 large egg

1 teaspoon vanilla extract

2 tablespoons heavy cream

2 cups coarsely chopped walnuts

¼ cup mini semisweet chocolate chips

Sea-salted Caramel Drizzle (page 180), for serving

To make the pastry dough, combine the cream cheese and butter in a bowl and beat with an electric mixer for about 1 minute. Add the flour, cocoa, sugar, and salt and mix on medium speed just until a dough begins to form and the ingredients are incorporated. Use your hands to pat the dough together in the bowl, folding it over on itself a few times to mix in any flour that remains on the surface. Form it into a ball, then flatten it into a disk, wrap it tightly in plastic wrap, and chill it in the refrigerator for at least 1 hour. (The dough can be made 1 day ahead and kept tightly wrapped in the refrigerator. Let sit at room temperature for 10 to 20 minutes to soften.)

To form the pastry cups, lightly dust the dough with flour on both sides and roll it out between 2 sheets of parchment paper to a thickness of about ⅛ inch. Use a 2½-inch round cutter to cut about 3 dozen rounds. Carefully transfer the dough rounds to the muffin cups and use a small pastry tamper or your fingers to mold the dough into the cups (if you are using your fingers, use a light touch to press the dough evenly across the bottom of each cup and up the sides). Transfer the pans to the refrigerator to keep the dough cold while you prepare the filling. (You can do this 1 day ahead, wrap tightly, and keep refrigerated—or double-wrap and freeze for up to 1 month, then fill and bake without thawing, adding an extra minute or two to the baking time.)

Preheat the oven to 350°F with two racks positioned in the upper and lower thirds of the oven.

To make the filling, combine the sugar and melted butter in a medium bowl and beat with an electric mixer on medium-high speed until smooth and creamy. Add the egg and beat well. Stir in the vanilla and cream, then fold in the walnuts.

Sprinkle approximately ½ teaspoon mini chocolate morsels into each of the chilled pastry shells. Use a mini scoop, melon baller, or teaspoon to top the chocolate chips with enough nut-and-sugar mixture to come level with the edge of the dough. Lightly press the filling down to settle it into the shell and fill in any gaps with a little more of the walnut mixture (the thick filling will rise only slightly when it bakes; you want the cups full but not overflowing).

Bake 10 to 12 minutes, or until the filling is golden brown, rotating the pans halfway through the baking time.

Set the pans on wire racks. Cool for about 5 minutes. While the tartlettini are still slightly warm, run the tip of a very sharp paring knife around the top edge to make sure the pastry hasn't adhered to the pan. Then let cool completely to room temperature before using the little knife to gently ease the tartlets out of the pan.

Transfer the tartlettini to a baking sheet or work surface lined with parchment and drizzle with the salted caramel. Serve at room temperature.

The tartlettini can be kept in an airtight container at room temperature for several days or frozen for up to 3 months (thaw at room temperature before serving).

Itty Bitty Pecan Pies

Here's my take on the traditional pecan pie: itty bitty tartlets with delicate crust and scrumptious-but-not-too-sweet filling that's laced with Amaretto and orange. Puts *un po 'di qualcosa di qualcosa* (a little somethin'-somethin') *Italiano* in an all-American classic. And you won't believe how easy it is to make.

· MAKES ABOUT 3 DOZEN ·

CREAM CHEESE PASTRY

4 ounces cream cheese, at room temperature

4 ounces (1 stick) unsalted butter, at room temperature

1 cup all-purpose flour

¼ teaspoon fine sea salt

PECAN FILLING

4 tablespoons (½ stick) unsalted butter, melted and cooled to room temperature

¼ teaspoon fine sea salt

½ cup packed light brown sugar

½ cup light corn syrup

1 teaspoon vanilla extract

1 tablespoon finely grated orange zest

1 tablespoon Amaretto

1 large egg, beaten

1½ cups chopped pecans

36 pecan halves

To make the pastry, combine the cream cheese and butter in a bowl and beat with an electric mixer for about 1 minute. Add the flour and salt and mix on medium speed just until a dough begins to form and the ingredients are incorporated. Flour your hands and pat the dough together in the bowl, folding it over on itself a few times to mix in any flour that remains on the surface. Form it into a ball, then flatten it into a disk, wrap it tightly in wax paper, and chill it in the refrigerator for at least 1 hour. (The pastry can be made 1 day ahead and kept tightly wrapped in the refrigerator. Let sit at room temperature for 10 to 20 minutes to soften.)

To form the pastry cups, on a lightly floured work surface roll the chilled dough out to a thickness of about ⅛ inch. Use a 2½-inch round cutter to cut about 3 dozen rounds (reroll scraps as needed). Carefully transfer the dough rounds to the muffin cups and use a small pastry tamper or your fingers to mold the dough into the cups (if you are using your fingers, use a light touch to press the dough evenly across the bottom of each cup and up the sides). Transfer the pans to the refrigerator to keep the dough cold while you prepare the filling. (You can do this 1 day ahead; wrap tightly, and keep refrigerated—or double wrap and freeze for up to 1 month, then fill and bake without thawing, adding an extra minute or two to the baking time.)

Preheat the oven to 350°F with two racks positioned in the upper and lower thirds of the oven.

To make the filling, in a large bowl combine the butter, salt, and sugar and beat with an electric mixer on medium-high speed until smooth. Add the corn syrup, vanilla, orange zest, and Amaretto and continue mixing on medium-high until uniformly blended.

(Recipe continued on next page)

Electric mixer

Two heavyweight nonstick 24-cavity
mini muffin pans

2½-inch round cutter, or a glass,
can, or bowl with an opening of that
diameter

Small pastry tamper, optional

Beat in the egg. Transfer the filling to a large measuring cup with a spout.

Divide the chopped pecans evenly among the pastry shells. Pour in just enough of the filling so it comes not quite level with the top edge of the pastry shells. Top each pie with a pecan half.

Bake 10 to 12 minutes, or until the filling is golden brown.

Set the pans on wire racks. Cool for about 5 minutes. While the pies are still slightly warm, run the tip of a small sharp knife around the top edge to make sure any filling that has oozed out around the pastry doesn't adhere to the pan. Then let cool completely to room temperature before using the little knife to gently ease the pies out of the pan.

Pistachio-Apricot Mezzelune

Half-moons of tender pastry filled with a delectable combination of rich pistachios, tangy apricot, and fragrant spices, these are a nice little snack to nibble on anytime. Back in the day, my mom used to make little pockets like these and we'd munch away on them while we watched those great nighttime soaps we loved so much—*Dallas, Falcon Crest, Knot's Landing*—all those shows that counted as nighttime drama before the days of *The Real Housewives of New Jersey.*

FILLING

1 cup diced dried apricot

¾ cup orange juice

⅓ cup honey

2 tablespoons diced crystallized or candied ginger

3 cinnamon sticks

½ teaspoon ground cinnamon

¾ cup chopped pistachios

One recipe Rustica Pastry (page 178)

1 large egg white, for brushing

Coarse sugar, for sprinkling

Finely chopped pistachios, for sprinkling, optional

equipment

2 large baking sheets

3½-inch round cutter, or a glass, can, or bowl with an opening of that diameter

To make the filling, combine the apricots, orange juice, honey, ginger, and cinnamon sticks in a medium, heavy-bottom saucepan. Bring the mixture to a boil over medium-high heat, then immediately turn the heat down to low. Simmer until the apricots soften and all the liquid has been absorbed, 7 to 10 minutes. Carefully transfer the mixture to a bowl and let cool to room temperature, then remove the cinnamon sticks. In a separate, small bowl combine the ground cinnamon and chopped pistachios, tossing to coat, then mix in the apricot mixture until well combined. Set aside (or cover and store overnight in the refrigerator).

To roll out and cut the dough, lightly dust a smooth countertop with flour and roll each disk of the dough out to an even thickness of about ⅛ inch (not too thin or it will become difficult to handle and fall apart). Transfer each sheet of dough to a baking sheet, wrap tightly with plastic, and return to the refrigerator for 15 minutes or until you are ready to cut it into rounds for the pastries. (The dough can be kept in the refrigerator overnight or double-wrapped and frozen at this stage for up to 3 months. Defrost for 1 hour before using.)

Preheat the oven to 350°F with two racks positioned in the upper and lower thirds of the oven. Line 2 large baking sheets with parchment paper.

Use a 3½-inch cutter to cut each sheet of the chilled dough into about 12 rounds, rerolling any scraps. (The cut rounds can be tightly wrapped and refrigerated overnight or double-wrapped and frozen for 1 month.)

(Recipe continued on next page)

Divide the dough rounds between the two parchment-lined baking sheets. Onto the bottom half of each round, drop a rounded teaspoon of filling. Fold the top half of the dough over and seal the edge by pressing gently with a fork. Shape the little pouches into crescents or half-moons.

Beat the egg white with 1 tablespoon water. Lightly brush the pastries with egg wash and sprinkle with coarse sugar and chopped pistachios. (The pastry can be frozen on baking sheets, then transferred to freezer bags and kept frozen for up to 1 month. Bake without thawing, adding about 5 minutes to the baking time.)

Bake the pastries until lightly golden, about 12 to 15 minutes, rotating halfway through the baking time. Let cool 5 minutes before serving, or serve at room temperature.

Pignoli Baklawa Bites

I learned to make Lebanese *baklawa* (pronounced "bok-LAH-WAH" and similar to, but distinct from, Greek "baklava") from Rich's mom, in the traditional style, big trays of it cut into diamond shapes. It is hugely important for special occasions—no Lebanese Christmas would be complete without baklawa. For smaller, tidier portions, I adapted Rich's mom's recipe to make little rolls. And because pine nuts are my and Rich's favorite, and a common ingredient in both Italian and Lebanese cooking, I use them rather than the more typical walnuts or pistachios. Pine nuts can be pricey, but for us they are the perfect buttery yet delicate nut for this buttery yet delicate dessert. Working with phyllo is a little tricky at first—keeping the papery dough covered at all times to prevent it from drying out, lightly brushing each piece with butter as you work with it to keep it pliable, rolling each cylinder tightly and placing them snugly together in the baking pan so they don't puff and unfurl, and working quickly to get the whole batch assembled and into the oven—but you soon get the hang of it and find that it's not difficult, just time-consuming. And the results are so worth it: a very generous batch of delicate, rich, and buttery but not overly sweet delights that keep for weeks and work a bit of magic on everyone you share them with.

• MAKES ABOUT 4 DOZEN •

PASTRY

One 1-pound box Apollo brand #7 phyllo pastry sheets, defrosted overnight in the refrigerator then brought to room temperature (important note: leave it in the package with the inner plastic wrapping intact while thawing)

1 pound (4 sticks) unsalted butter (to make clarified butter)

PIGNOLI FILLING

3 cups pine nuts

¼ cup granulated sugar

1 teaspoon *mazaher* (orange blossom water)

Orange Blossom Syrup (page 179)

To make the clarified butter, slowly melt the butter in a heavy-bottom saucepan over low heat. After about 5 minutes it will begin to bubble and foam. Skim off the foam. Take the pan off the heat and let the butter settle for 3 to 5 minutes. The milky solids will sink to the bottom of the pan. Carefully pour off the clear liquid into a container, leaving the solids behind (discard the solids). (The clarified butter can be made ahead; it will keep in an airtight container in the refrigerator for months.)

To make the nut filling, use a food processor fitted with the standard blade to finely grind the pine nuts. (Don't over-grind to the point of liquefying into a nut butter—just to fine bits. Pine nuts are very oily, so they will stick together but not quite form a paste.) Transfer the ground nuts to a large bowl. Add the sugar and mix well until uniformly combined. Add the *mazaher* and mix well.

(Recipe continued on next page)

Food processor

Large rimmed baking sheet, or square or rectangular casserole (I use a 10- x 15-inch baking pan, but any pan with a 1-inch rim is fine, even if there's extra room in the pan—just be sure to place the phyllo rolls together very snugly)

Pastry brush

Preheat the oven 325°F with a rack positioned in the center. Line the baking pan with parchment paper.

Unwrap and unroll the phyllo dough, leaving the sheets stacked together on top of the plastic wrapping (even if you end up cutting through it, having the phyllo on the plastic makes it easier to move it around and helps keep it from drying out). Lay the sheets flat on a large cutting board. Use a ruler or straight edge and a large knife to cut the sheets in thirds lengthwise. (Different brands vary a bit in the number and size of sheets in each package. I use Apollo brand, which has 16 sheets about 14 by 18 inches, so when I cut the sheets in 3 equal strips I have 48 strips that are each about 4¾ inches wide. If your package has more or fewer sheets and/or they are a somewhat different size, the recipe will still work just fine—you'll just get a different number of rolls of a somewhat different size.)

Immediately cover the stack of phyllo strips loosely with a sheet of plastic wrap topped with a slightly damp, clean kitchen towel and keep it covered until you have finished assembling the baklawa. (This is important: phyllo is paper-thin and tends to dry out very quickly, so it must always be covered.)

Carefully take a single phyllo strip at a time and lay it down on a flat surface, with one of the short sides facing you. Brush the phyllo strip lightly with clarified butter. Place a tablespoon of sugared nuts about 2½ to 3 inches above the bottom edge of the strip. Mound the nuts into a small rounded log approximately 2 inches wide and parallel to the bottom edge of the phyllo strip. Fold the bottom edge of phyllo up and over the nuts and roll tightly a few times, taking care not to tear the dough. Fold in the outer edges of the strip, tuck them in, and continue rolling the remaining length of the strip, brushing on a little more butter as needed to help the dough stay barely moist. (You will end up with a little cylinder about 3 inches long and 1 inch in diameter.) Set the roll seam-side down on the prepared baking sheet, placing it snugly in the corner of the pan. Repeat with the remaining 47 strips of phyllo, placing them tightly together in the baking pan (don't leave space in between or they will puff and loosen—but if there is space in the pan the rolls on the outer edge will be just fine, so long as you roll them nice and tight, place them seam-side down in the pan, and snug them up against the other rolls on one side). Brush the rolls with the remaining butter (or just pour over top).

Bake 30 to 35 minutes, or just until lightly golden. Do not overbake.

Remove the pan from the oven and immediately—but slowly—pour the syrup all over the pastry, distributing it evenly.

Allow the baklawa to cool completely in the pan (it will absorb the syrup), then transfer to a serving tray; or store at room temperature, covered loosely with wax paper or foil (don't wrap tightly or they will get soggy) and keep in a cool place for up to 2 weeks.

---

important: phyllo comes in a range of thicknesses. I use Apollo brand #7 sheets, which are a medium thickness. There is also a #10 thickness, which is extra thick. I've found that other brands vary widely in thickness and some are so thin that they're difficult to work with, especially if you are new to phyllo.

note: *Mazaher* (orange blossom water) is distilled from the petals of orange blossoms and it is a key ingredient in Lebanese baklawa, giving the pastry an amazing, subtle, and uplifting perfume. *Mazaher* is sold at Middle Eastern markets and many large supermarkets. You can also order it online.

Petite Pumpkin
Pies with Toasted
Mashmallow Topping

page {46}

Now That's Using Your *Googootz!*

When Rosie and I were growing up, we always painted the faces on our jack-o'-lanterns. "Why," my thrifty and practical mother would say, "would we waste a perfectly good pumpkin by cutting a face in it and putting it out to rot?" After Halloween we would wash the paint off the pumpkins, cut them up, and cook up all kinds of wonderful dishes. Mom certainly wasn't depriving us, she was just using her *googootz*—literally! I should explain: *googootz* is an Italian-American term for various kinds of squash. Also, all my life I'd also hear my uncles and a lot of the older uncle-like guys who were always around use the word mockingly, when teasing someone for being empty-headed, as in "Don't be a big *googootz!*" In other words, a big pumpkin head.

Having raised two kids in suburban New Jersey, I have carved many jack-o'-lanterns, and I long ago discovered the wonders of baking with canned pumpkin purée (though I do love cooking with fresh roasted pumpkin and by all means encourage you to use it in any of the following recipes—just be sure to purée it very finely).

Pumpkin Spice Babycakes

If there's an easier and tastier recipe for homemade cake than this, I haven't found it yet. It's the kind of treat you can throw together on the fly, without planning or shopping ahead, as long as you have the most basic baking staples and some pumpkin purée on hand (it's one of those canned items that seems to take up residence in the cupboard, know what I mean?). The fragrant little cakes are so moist and delicious, you really could go without the mascarpone frosting. But don't get me wrong; I'm not saying you should go without the frosting . . . it is divinely creamy, super-easy, and dresses up the quick little cakes beautifully.

• MAKES ABOUT 3 DOZEN •

PUMPKIN SPICE BABYCAKES

1¼ cups all-purpose flour

1½ teaspoons pumpkin pie spice

¾ teaspoon baking soda

¼ teaspoon baking powder

½ teaspoon fine sea salt

6 tablespoons unsalted butter, at room temperature

¾ cup packed dark brown sugar

2 large eggs

¼ cup orange juice

1½ teaspoons vanilla extract

1 cup pure pumpkin purée

Mascarpone Frosting (page 43)

equipment

Two heavyweight nonstick 24-cavity mini muffin pans

Pastry bag and large star tip

Preheat the oven to 350°F with two racks positioned in the upper and lower thirds of the oven. Grease the mini muffin pans.

In a large bowl, sift together the flour, pumpkin pie spice, baking soda, baking powder, and sea salt.

In a separate large bowl, cream together the butter and sugar. Add the eggs, orange juice, and vanilla and beat to combine. Then add the pumpkin and mix well. (The batter will look very unappealing at this point—no worries!)

Stir in the flour mixture just until incorporated.

Spoon the batter into the pans, filling 36 of the cavities about two-thirds of the way to the rim.

Bake 8 to 10 minutes, or until the tops of the cakes are evenly browned and spring back when gently pressed with a finger, rotating the pans front to back and top to bottom halfway through the baking time. Set the pans on wire racks and let the cakes cool to room temperature before easing them out of the cups.

Cut the cakes in half crosswise and use a piping bag fitted with a star tip to fill with frosting. Pipe a little star of frosting onto the center of the tops to give them a pretty finishing touch. Chill to set, about 1 hour, then let sit 30 minutes at room temperature before serving.

tip: One cup pure pumpkin purée is half of a 15-ounce can of pumpkin purée. You can double the recipe to use the entire can all at once, but you can also freeze the leftover purée: transfer it to a zip-top freezer bag and squeeze out as much air as possible before sealing. Thaw before using to make another round of babycakes—or step it up to the sticky buns (page 45)!

Mascarpone Frosting *Makes about 2½ cups*

4 ounces cream cheese, at room temperature

4 ounces (1 stick) unsalted butter, cut into tablespoons and softened

2 cups confectioners' sugar

1 teaspoon vanilla extract

One 8-ounce tub mascarpone, at room temperature

equipment

Electric mixer

Combine the cream cheese, butter, and sugar in a large bowl and blend with a mixer on low speed until the sugar is incorporated, then switch the machine to medium-high and beat until light and creamy, 2 to 3 minutes. Add the vanilla extract and beat to incorporate.

Pour off any water that has separated out of the mascarpone. Add the mascarpone to the bowl and beat on low just until incorporated (take care not to overbeat, or you'll have grainy frosting).

Use immediately or refrigerate for up to 1 week (bring to room temperature before using).

Pumpkin Spice Baby Bundts

Double the batter for the Pumpkin Spice Babycakes (page 42), add a layer of super simple filling, and you have a lovely seasonal treat. Add maple brown butter glaze and you have an even lovelier, even more perfectly autumnal treat—and you may also get a standing ovation.

· MAKES 2 DOZEN ·

FILLING

1 cup sweetened dried cranberries, coarsely chopped

1 cup toasted walnuts, coarsely chopped

¼ cup packed light brown sugar

1 teaspoon cinnamon

½ teaspoon nutmeg

Double recipe Pumpkin Spice Babycakes batter (page 42)

Maple–Brown Butter Glaze (below)

equipment

Two 12-cavity, heavyweight, nonstick mini Bundt pans (preferably fluted)

Preheat the oven to 350°F with two racks positioned in the upper and lower thirds of the oven. Grease two 12-cavity mini Bundt pans.

In a medium bowl, combine the cranberries, nuts, light brown sugar, cinnamon, and nutmeg and stir well to combine. Set aside.

Prepare the batter as directed for Pumpkin Spice Babycakes.

Spoon 3 tablespoons of the batter into each Bundt, spreading evenly. Top each with 2 tablespoons of the cranberry nut mixture followed by another 3 tablespoons batter, filling to about ¼ inch below of the rim of the pan.

Bake 12 to 15 minutes, or until the tops of the cakes are evenly browned and spring back when gently pressed with a finger, rotating the pans front to back and top to bottom halfway through the baking time. Cool to room temperature on wire racks.

Turn the cooled cakes out of the pans and set them on a parchment-lined baking sheet. Drizzle with the glaze and leave at room temperature (or refrigerate briefly) until the glaze is set.

Maple–Brown Butter Glaze *Makes about 3 cups*

4 ounces (1 stick) unsalted butter

1½ cups confectioners' sugar

½ cup maple syrup

Heat the butter in a small saucepan over medium-high heat until it turns a deep golden brown color, about 5 minutes. Pour the browned butter through a fine-mesh strainer into a bowl, discarding any dark sediment. Whisk in the confectioners' sugar until combined, followed by the maple syrup. Use immediately.

Pumpkin Ginger Pecan Sticky Buns

There is a reason that sticky buns are almost never homemade. All of the recipes I've ever tried for sticky buns (all the good ones anyway) require making a yeast dough that has to rise—*twice*. Now, I am a lady who makes her own cannoli, including the shells, from scratch, but I can't hack double-rising dough (we all have our limits!). So how excited was I when my experiment with itsy bitsy upside-down pumpkin babycakes came out tasting for all the world like the best damn sticky buns I've ever had? What a happy surprise. And they are *easy*. Enjoy!

•MAKES ABOUT 3 DOZEN•

¼ cup crystallized ginger, very finely chopped

½ cup pecans, finely chopped

1 recipe Pumpkin Spice Babycakes batter (page 42)

¾ cup Caramel Drizzle (page 180)

equipment

Two heavyweight nonstick 24-cavity mini muffin pans

Preheat the oven to 350°F with two racks positioned in the upper and lower thirds of the oven. Generously butter the mini muffin pans.

Combine the ginger and pecans in a small bowl and use your fingers to mix until thoroughly combined. Set aside.

Prepare the batter as directed for Pumpkin Spice Babycakes.

Prepare the Caramel Drizzle.

Spoon (or better yet, use a squeeze bottle to dispense) about 1 teaspoon caramel into about 3 dozen of the wells in the prepared pans. Add 1 teaspoon of the ginger pecan mixture, then spoon in about 1 tablespoon of the batter, filling each cavity to within about ¼ inch of the pan rim.

Bake 8 to 10 minutes, or until the tops of the cakes are evenly browned and spring back when gently pressed with a finger, rotating the pans front to back and top to bottom halfway through the baking time. Cool on wire racks for a few minutes, then, while the sticky buns are still quite warm, use an offset spatula or a butter knife to ease the sticky buns out of the pan. (Turning the buns out before they've cooled off will help prevent the topping from adhering to the bottom of the pan, but if some does stick, don't despair; just scoop it out and stick it back on top of the bun while still warm.)

Serve, gooey nutty sides up, at room temperature.

Petite Pumpkin Pies with Toasted Marshmallow Topping

For a lot of people it's just not Thanksgiving without a casserole of candied sweet potatoes covered in marshmallows. That has never been my thing, maybe because I didn't grow up having it. But I do adore pumpkin pie, and here's my new favorite way to serve it: a simple, deliciously flaky crust (individual minis, of course) brimming with an ultra-classic filling (softly spiced and super silky), topped with a beautiful cloud of homemade marshmallow cream. Talk about a crowd-pleaser!

—•MAKES 2 DOZEN•—

CRUST

3⅓ cups all-purpose flour

½ teaspoon cinnamon

½ teaspoon ground ginger

¼ teaspoon freshly grated nutmeg

¾ teaspoon fine sea salt

11 ounces (2⅔ sticks) cold unsalted butter, cut into ½-inch cubes

⅓ cup ice water, plus more if needed

1 egg white, for brushing

Coarse sugar, for sprinkling

FILLING

One 15-ounce can pure pumpkin purée (2 cups)

4 large eggs

1 cup packed light brown sugar

½ teaspoon cinnamon

½ teaspoon ground ginger

½ teaspoon freshly grated nutmeg

1 cup evaporated milk

Combine the flour, cinnamon, ginger, nutmeg, and salt in the bowl of a food processor fitted with the standard blade and pulse to combine. Add the butter and pulse until the mixture resembles very coarse cornmeal (just a few 1-second pulses). Add ⅓ cup ice water, then pulse the machine a few more times. Add more ice water 1 teaspoon at a time, pulsing only enough to combine the ingredients—just until the mixture begins to gather together, but not long enough to allow it to form a ball.

Turn the dough out onto a large sheet of plastic wrap. Lightly pat the pieces together through the paper. Split the dough into 2 equal portions, pat each into a thick flat disk, wrap tightly, and refrigerate until well chilled, at least 2 hours. (The dough can be tightly wrapped and refrigerated overnight or double-wrapped and frozen for 1 month.)

On a smooth, lightly floured work surface, roll out 1 of the chilled disks of dough to an even thickness of about ⅛ inch. Use a 4¾- to 5-inch cutter to cut out 6 circles of dough, rerolling the scraps as needed. (The dough circles can be layered with parchment or wax paper, wrapped tightly in plastic, and refrigerated for up to 2 days; or double-wrapped and frozen for up to 1 month.)

Carefully transfer the dough circles to the tartlet pans, pressing gently with a pastry tamper or your fingers to mold the dough to the pan. Each circle should have an overhang of about ¼ inch

Marshmallow Cream (page 186)

equipment

Food processor

Fluted mini tart pans measuring 3½ inches across the top, 2 inches across the bottom, and 1 inch deep, or as close to these dimensions as possible

4¾- to 5-inch round cutter, or a glass, can, or bowl with an opening of that diameter

Small pastry tamper, optional

Two large rimmed baking sheets

of dough above the edge of the pan. Roll out the second disk of dough and cut it into more rounds, rerolling scraps as needed to make all 12.

To make a fluted edge, turn the overhanging dough under to form a rolled edge, then crimp by pinching it at ½-inch intervals between your thumb and bent finger and pushing forward on a slant with your finger while pulling back with your thumb. Freeze until firm, about 15 minutes.

While the dough chills, preheat the oven to 425°F and cut twelve 5-inch circles of parchment. Line the chilled crusts with the parchment and fill with uncooked rice or dried uncooked beans (this will weigh down the crusts while they prebake and prevent them from shrinking). Set the tartlet pans on rimmed baking sheets and bake 10 minutes. Lift out the parchment and rice or beans (which can be kept in a jar and re-used for the same purpose), and bake 5 more minutes, or just until lightly browned all over. Set the trays of prebaked crusts aside to cool on wire racks.

Turn oven temperature down to 350°F.

To make the filling, combine the pumpkin, eggs, sugar, spices, and evaporated milk in a large bowl and whisk together until well combined.

Divide the filling among the prebaked crusts, filling each level with the top edge. Set the pans on rimmed baking sheets and bake for 25 minutes, or just until the edges are set but the center is still slightly jiggly, rotating from top to bottom and front to back halfway through the baking time.

Set the baking sheets on wire racks and let the pies cool completely to room temperature. (Best to make at least 1 day ahead and store at room temperature, loosely covered with foil. It's important to cool before adding marshmallow topping, so it doesn't melt from bottom up before getting toasted on top.)

Preheat the broiler to low, with a rack positioned in the center of the oven.

(Recipe continued on next page)

Top each pie with a generous dollop of marshmallow cream, swirling decoratively. Transfer the pies on the baking sheets back into the oven for about 1 minute, just until the marshmallow topping is lightly toasted.

Cool to room temperature before serving—best to make at least 1 day ahead (the same is true for all pies), and could be made up to 3 days in advance. If so, refrigerate, but not too tightly covered so crusts don't get soggy, then bring to room temperature before serving.

Holiday Treat Tray

I love the holidays and all the baking that comes with the territory. I enjoy putting a tray of home-baked goodies out after dinner and just sitting around talking over a cup of coffee or two. I also like taking things I've baked to people's houses as gifts or as part of a potluck supper. Everybody loves them—I mean, who doesn't like getting treats? There are many treats from this book that you could put on a holiday treat tray (I like to decorate my treat trays with sprigs of pine and holly, plus maybe a Christmas ornament to keep things festive). Below is a short list I've gathered based on a few rules I follow when I'm making up a holiday tray: All of the treats must be good make-aheads that keep well and/or can be frozen. There must be something festive about them. And, most important, they must be extraordinarily yummy. Here's a list of some of my favorites that meet all of those criteria:

Pignoli Bites (page 37)

Caramel Chocolate Walnut Tartlettini (page 28)

Itty Bitty Pecan Pies (page 31)

Fresh Fig Borsettini (page 9)

Tiramisu Tradizionale (page 151)

Pistachio-Apricot Mezzelune (page 33)

Figs in Baskets (page 11)

Pumpkin Ginger Pecan Sticky Buns (page 45)

Blueberry Streusel Baby Bundts (page 85)

Chocolate Babycakes (page 76)

White Chocolate Blondie Bites (page 113)

Beach Baby Blondies (page 114)

Bitsy Brunettes (page 116)

Chocolate-Chili Brownie Bites (page 117)

Wintertime really brings out the hostess in me. The cold weather and short days mean there is so much less going out and about, so much more gathering in and cozying up. It's a great time for dinner parties, with hearty comforting foods and lingering hours of conversation at the table, eventually making way for some decadent little desserts.

Then there's the special family time that winter brings, which I have treasured since I was a little girl. Fond memories of building igloos and snowmen with my little sister, Rosie, and my big brothers Ralph, Joe, and Anthony (they're not on the show but I do have them—my eldest brother Ralph is almost a decade older than I am, so Rosie and I kinda grew up like a little second generation of girls) always warm my heart when I see the snow start to fall.

Christmastime in my house has always been so special. From as far back as I can remember, my mom and I would start planning which cookies to make early on. There were the traditional staples we always made (sprinkle cookies, sugar cookies, *struffoli*, etc.) and then new varieties we'd play with from year to year (jam thumbprints, biscotti, pignoli cookies). Being who I am, when I started baking on my own I took it to another level, adding decadent things like cheesecake, tiramisu, fruit tarts, pecan pie, and so on. And the leftovers I had! Once I started doing individual portion-sized treats, it made it easier to freeze some of everything to serve

throughout the season—plus it made everything pretty enough to share (unlike a whole pie or cake once a slice has been cut out of it).

Holidays aside, just in the day-to-day course of things, the cold weather keeps us inside together so much more. As a child my winters were full of indoor projects and hobbies and crafts with my mom and my sister. A lot of my early learning in the kitchen with my mom happened in the wintertime. A weekend afternoon of baking treats and playing endless games of rummy 500—that was the best. And one of the great joys of being a mom has been baking projects with my daughter, Victoria, and my son, Joseph (who is crazy for sweets like his mom and has always loved baking with me). They are just about all grown up now, but we still do a lot of baking together in the winter and love to settle in with our sweet treats, piling onto the couch with Rich to watch movies. These days even though our movie preferences are so different we can always agree on a great suspense-filled drama.

*Lemon Dream
Cheesecake Cuties*

page {56}

For the Love of Cheesecake

Cheesecake was my gateway recipe—the first serious dessert I learned to make and then made my own. I don't remember what exactly inspired me to make a project out of cracking the cheesecake code, I just know that I spent a whole lot of my free time during freshman year in high school in my mom's kitchen baking cheesecake after cheesecake after cheesecake. I tried out every cheesecake recipe I could get my hands on—off of cream cheese, ricotta, and graham cracker packages, and from old issues of *Ladies' Home Journal* that I'd page through on slow days at the hair salon where I worked as a shampoo girl, plus recipes I would get from clients.

There were a lot of mediocre cheesecakes along the way, and a few flat-out fails. In those days I relied on my big brothers for cheesecake critiques. (It's funny how all four of my siblings worked in restaurants but none of them ever took much of an interest in baking. Maybe I cornered that market in my family. Anyhow, they sure did enjoy the sweets I made—and still do! Especially Ralph and Anthony, who both inherited our dad's sweet tooth.)

Eventually I got the cheesecake fundamentals just right: the perfect balance of creamy yet ethereal, sweet with the faintest whisper of tanginess. That is the origin of the classic cheesecake I make to this day, and the basis for the many spinoffs I've created over the years (three of my faves are included here).

If you think you don't like cheesecake, I am willing to bet it's because you've never had it the way it ought to be. And if you have had the good fortune to experience great cheesecake but don't make it yourself because it has a reputation for being complicated, forget that. Either way, try these recipes—they take some time and close attention but are so worth it!

Classic Cheesecake Cuties

Many traditional recipes call for cooking cheesecake in a water bath to keep the filling moist and prevent the tops from cracking. For mini cheesecakes I've found that it is a whole lot easier and just as effective to put a pan of water in the bottom of the oven when you preheat.

•MAKES 2 DOZEN•

CRUST

1¼ cups graham cracker crumbs

4 tablespoons (½ stick) unsalted butter, melted

TOPPING

½ cup sour cream

3 tablespoons granulated sugar

1 teaspoon vanilla extract

FILLING

Two 8-ounce packages cream cheese, at room temperature

½ cup granulated sugar

1 tablespoon all-purpose flour

3 large eggs

3 tablespoons heavy cream

3 tablespoons sour cream

1 tablespoon vanilla extract

Fresh fruit, for serving

equipment

Two 12-cavity mini cheesecake pans

Small pastry tamper, optional

Electric mixer

Two large rimmed baking sheets

Preheat the oven to 350°F with one rack positioned in the center of the oven and another rack positioned at the bottom of the oven. Fill a broiler pan or roasting pan with about 2 inches of water and set it on the bottom rack.

To make the crust, combine the graham cracker crumbs and melted butter in a medium bowl, mixing until the ingredients are combined and the crumbs are thoroughly moistened with the butter. Scoop about 1 tablespoon of the crumb mixture into each cavity in the mini cheesecake pan and use a pastry tamper, a small spoon, or the back of a small melon ball scoop to spread the mixture evenly and press it firmly into place. Transfer the pans to the refrigerator to chill the crust while you prepare the topping and the filling.

To make the topping, combine the sour cream, sugar, and vanilla in a small bowl and mix thoroughly. Reserve in the refrigerator.

To make the filling, in a large bowl beat together the cream cheese, sugar, and flour with a mixer at medium speed until smooth and creamy. Beat in each egg separately and scrape down the bowl after each addition. Continue mixing at medium speed and add the heavy cream, sour cream, and vanilla.

Set the cheesecake pans on rimmed baking sheets (this will make it easier to get them in and out of the oven). Transfer the filling to a large measuring cup with a spout and pour enough filling into each cavity of the pans to fill a bit more than three-quarters of the way up to the rim.

Bake for 7 minutes at 350°F, then lower the temperature to 250°F and bake 10 to 12 more minutes, or just until the surfaces of the cuties are set at the outer edges but still wobbly in the center. (Keep a close eye on them!)

Take the pans out of the oven and divide the sour cream topping among the cakes, spooning an even layer onto each and smoothing out the tops with the back of the spoon. Return the pans to the oven and bake for an additional 7 minutes. (They'll still look wet, but they will set as they cool.)

Let the cakes cool in the pans for 3 to 5 minutes, then run the tip of a very sharp knife around the top edge of each cake (this will unstick any topping that has adhered to the side of the pan and help the cake come out of the pan easily and flawlessly once they are cool.) *Don't try to unmold the cakes while they are still warm!*

Let the cuties cool in the pans all the way to room temperature, at least 30 minutes. Carefully unmold the cooled cuties by pressing the little round disk beneath each cake upward to raise the cake so that its bottom is level with the pan rim, then slide a small spatula underneath the cake and transfer the cake to a storage container or serving dish. Cover and refrigerate at least 6 hours before serving.

Serve cold, topped with your favorite fresh fruit, or Raspberry Drizzle (page 182).

These can be kept refrigerated in an airtight container for 3 to 5 days, or frozen for up to 3 months (thaw overnight in the refrigerator or for 1 hour at room temperature before serving).

Lemon Dream Cheesecake Cuties

Lusciously lemon-dreamy from top to bottom, these cuties have buttery pine nuts in the crust. Chop the pine nuts finely, almost but not quite to a paste (once ground they will be quite oily.) Also among the many charms of these citrusy cuties are the pockets of sweet-tart lemon in the centers. I always make the lemon curd ahead of time to simplify the process of preparing the cheesecakes.

• MAKES 2 DOZEN •

CRUST

1¼ cups vanilla wafer crumbs (approximately 1½ cups mini vanilla wafers)

¼ cup pine nuts, lightly toasted and finely chopped (preferably in a food processor)

1 teaspoon finely grated lemon zest

4 tablespoons (½ stick) unsalted butter, melted

TOPPING

½ cup sour cream

3 tablespoons granulated sugar

1 teaspoon vanilla extract

1 teaspoon lemon extract

FILLING

Two 8-ounce packages cream cheese, at room temperature

½ cup granulated sugar

3 large eggs

3 tablespoons heavy cream

3 tablespoons sour cream

1 teaspoon vanilla extract

1 teaspoon lemon extract

1 teaspoon finely grated lemon zest

1 recipe Lemon Curd (page 183)

Preheat the oven to 350°F with one rack positioned in the center of the oven and another rack positioned at the bottom of the oven. Fill a broiler pan or roasting pan with about 2 inches of water and set it on the bottom rack.

To make the crust, combine the cookie crumbs, pine nuts, lemon zest, and melted butter in a medium bowl, mixing until the ingredients are combined and the crumbs are thoroughly moistened with the butter.

Scoop about 1 tablespoon of the crumb mixture into each cavity in the mini cheesecake pan and use a pastry tamper, small spoon, or the back of a small melon ball scoop to spread the mixture evenly and press firmly into place. Transfer the pans to the refrigerator to chill the crusts while you prepare the topping and the filling.

To make the topping, combine the sour cream, sugar, and the vanilla and lemon extracts in a small bowl and mix thoroughly. Reserve in the refrigerator.

To make the filling, in a large bowl beat together the cream cheese and sugar with an electric mixer at medium speed until smooth. Beat in each egg separately and scrape down the bowl after each addition. Continue to mix at medium speed and add the heavy cream, sour cream, vanilla and lemon extracts, and lemon zest.

Set the cheesecake pans on rimmed baking sheets (this will make it easier to get them in and out of the oven). Center a small dollop (a rounded teaspoon) of lemon curd on each crust, taking care that the curd does not touch the sides of the pan, Transfer the filling to a large measuring cup with a spout and pour enough filling into the cavity of each pan to fill about three-quarters of the way up the rim.

Freshly whipped heavy cream, for garnish

Fresh mint sprigs, for garnish

Long thin strips of lemon zest, for garnish

equipment

Two 12-cavity mini cheesecake pans

Small pastry tamper, optional

Electric mixer

Two large rimmed baking sheets

Bake for 7 minutes at 350°F, then lower the temperature to 250°F and bake 10 to 12 more minutes, or just until the surfaces of the cuties are set at the outer edges but still wobbly in the center. (Keep a close eye on them!)

Take the pans out of the oven and divide the sour cream topping among the cakes, spooning an even layer onto each and smoothing out the tops with the back of the spoon. Return the pans to the oven and bake for an additional 7 minutes. (They'll still look wet, but they will set as they cool.)

Let the cakes cool in the pans for 3 to 5 minutes, then run the tip of a very sharp knife around the top edge of each cake (this will unstick any topping that has adhered to the side of the pan and help the cake come out of the pan easily and flawlessly once they are cool.) *Don't try to unmold the cakes while they are still warm!*

Let the cuties cool in the pans all the way to room temperature, at least 30 minutes. Carefully unmold the cooled cuties by pressing the little round disk beneath each cake upward to raise the cake so that its bottom is level with the pan rim, then slide a small spatula underneath the cake and transfer the cake to a storage container or serving dish. Cover and refrigerate at least 6 hours before serving. Top each cutie with a small dollop of freshly whipped cream, a little sprig of fresh mint, and a curlicue of lemon zest.

These can be kept refrigerated in an airtight container for 3 to 5 days, or frozen for up to 3 months (thaw overnight in the refrigerator or for 1 hour at room temperature before serving).

Chocolate Cheesecake Cuties

With a chocolate wafer crust, rich chocolate filling, and silky cocoa–cream topping, these are a chocolate lover's delight—one that can easily be made gluten-free by using gluten-free chocolate wafers. Top with whatever kind of nuts you like—I happen to love walnuts with this.

•MAKES 2 DOZEN•

CRUST

1⅓ cups chocolate wafer cookie crumbs (approximately 28 wafers)

4 tablespoons unsalted butter, melted

TOPPING

½ cup sour cream

3 tablespoons granulated sugar

3 tablespoons unsweetened cocoa powder

1 teaspoon vanilla extract

FILLING

One 4-ounce bar semisweet chocolate, finely chopped

3 tablespoons heavy cream

Two 8-ounce packages cream cheese, at room temperature

½ cup granulated sugar

2 large eggs

3 tablespoons sour cream

1 tablespoon vanilla extract

Chopped toasted nuts, for garnish

Chantilly Cream (page 183), for garnish

Chocolate shavings, for garnish

Preheat the oven to 350°F with one rack positioned in the center of the oven and another rack positioned at the bottom of the oven. Fill a broiler pan or roasting pan with about 2 inches of water and set it on the bottom rack.

To make the crust, combine the cookie crumbs and melted butter in a medium bowl, gently mixing until the crumbs are thoroughly moistened with the butter. Scoop about 1 tablespoon of the crumb mixture into each cavity in the mini cheesecake pan and use a pastry tamper, small spoon, or the back of a small melon ball scoop to spread evenly and press firmly into place. Transfer the pans to the refrigerator to chill the crust while you prepare the topping and the filling.

To make the cocoa topping, combine the sour cream, sugar, cocoa powder, and vanilla in a small bowl and mix thoroughly. Reserve in the refrigerator.

To make the filling, combine the chopped chocolate and the cream in a small heatproof bowl and set over a small saucepan of simmering water. Stir often until the chocolate is melted and the mixture is combined and very smooth. Set aside to cool completely to room temperature.

In a separate bowl, beat together the cream cheese and sugar with an electric mixer at medium speed until smooth and creamy. Beat in each egg separately and scrape down the bowl after each addition. Continue to mix at medium speed and add the sour cream and the vanilla. Add the cooled chocolate and blend well, using a flexible spatula to scrape down the sides and bottom of the bowl so that all the chocolate gets incorporated uniformly.

Set the cheesecake pans on rimmed baking sheets (this will make it easier to get them in and out of the oven). Transfer the filling to a large measuring cup with a spout and pour enough filling into each cavity of the pans to fill a bit more than three-quarters of the way up to the rim.

Bake for 7 minutes at 350°F, then lower the temperature to 250°F and bake 10 to 12 more minutes, or just until the surfaces of the cuties are set at the outer edges but still wobbly in the center. (Keep a close eye on them!)

Take the pans out of the oven and divide the cocoa topping among the cuties, spooning an even layer onto each and smoothing out the tops with the back of the spoon. Return the pans to the oven and bake for an additional 7 minutes. (They'll still look wet, but they will set as they cool.)

Let the cakes cool in the pans for 3 to 5 minutes, then run the tip of a very sharp knife around the top edge of each cake (this will unstick any topping that has adhered to the side of the pan and help the cuties come out of the pan easily and flawlessly once they are cool.) *Don't try to unmold the cakes while they are still warm!*

Let the cuties cool in the pans all the way to room temperature, at least 30 minutes, then transfer them to the refrigerator and chill thoroughly, at least 1 hour. Carefully unmold the chilled cuties by pressing the little round disk beneath each cake upward to raise the cake so that its bottom is level with the pan rim, then slide a small spatula underneath the cake and transfer to a storage container or serving dish. Cover and refrigerate at least 6 hours before serving.

Serve cold, topped with chopped nuts and/or a dollop of fresh whipped cream and some chocolate shavings.

These can be kept refrigerated in an airtight container for 3 to 5 days, or frozen for up to 3 months (thaw overnight in the refrigerator or for 1 hour at room temperature before serving).

Be sure to chill the cakes in the pan for at least 1 hour before unmolding.

Almond Joyous Cheesecake Cuties

Inspired by the candy bar I loved as a kid (and still do), these superdecadent confections are one of my favorite desserts to share with friends and family who have to steer clear of gluten. (So yummy and totally gluten-free—believe it!) The ganache can be spread all over the top and sides of the cakes or simply drizzled over the top so that it drips down the sides.

•MAKES 2 DOZEN•

CRUST

2 large egg whites

¼ cup granulated sugar

2 cups sweetened flaked coconut

TOPPING

½ cup sour cream

3 tablespoons sugar

1 teaspoon almond extract

FILLING

Two 8-ounce packages cream cheese, at room temperature

½ cup granulated sugar

3 large eggs

3 tablespoons sour cream

3 tablespoons heavy cream

1 teaspoon almond extract

2 teaspoons coconut extract

¼ cup almonds, toasted and finely chopped

Ganache (page 181)

Sliced almonds, for garnish

Preheat the oven to 350°F with one rack positioned in the center of the oven and another rack positioned at the bottom of the oven. Fill a broiler pan or roasting pan with about 2 inches of water and set it on the bottom rack.

To make the crust, combine the egg whites with the sugar in a medium bowl and use an electric mixer to beat to very stiff peaks. Use a rubber spatula to fold in the coconut until well combined. Scoop about 1 tablespoon of the mixture into each cavity in the mini cheesecake pan and use the back of the measuring spoon to firmly compress the mixture into an even layer about ¼ inch thick. Set aside.

To make the almond topping, in a small bowl stir together the sour cream, sugar, and almond extract. Set aside.

To make the filling, in a separate bowl beat together the cream cheese and sugar with an electric mixer at medium speed until smooth and creamy. Beat in each egg separately and scrape down the bowl after each addition. Continue to mix at medium speed and add the sour cream, heavy cream, almond extract, and coconut extract.

Set the cheesecake pans on rimmed baking sheets (this will make it easier to get them in and out of the oven). Press the crust down again to ensure that it is well packed.

Transfer the filling to a large measuring cup with a spout and pour enough filling into each cavity of the pans to fill a bit more than three-quarters of the way up to the rim.

(Recipe continued on next page)

Bake for 7 minutes at 350°F then lower the temperature to 250°F and bake 10 to 12 more minutes, or just until the surfaces of the cuties are set at the outer edges but still wobbly in the center. (Keep a close eye on them!)

Take the pans out of the oven and divide the almond topping among the cakes, spooning an even layer onto each and smoothing the tops with the back of the spoon. Top with the chopped almonds, then return the pans to the oven and bake for an additional 7 minutes. (They'll still look wet, but they will set as they cool.)

Let the cakes cool in the pans for 3 to 5 minutes, then run the tip of a very sharp knife around the top edge of each cake (this will unstick any topping that has adhered to the side of the pan and help the cake come out of the pan easily and flawlessly once they are cool.) *Don't try to add the chocolate ganache or unmold the cakes while they are still warm!*

Let the cuties cool in the pans all the way to room temperature, at least 30 minutes. Then chill in pans for 2 hours before unmolding and topping with ganache.

Carefully unmold the cuties by pressing the little round disk underneath each cake upward to raise the cake so that its bottom is level with the pan rim, then slide a small spatula underneath the cake.

To cover the cuties with ganache, arrange the unmolded cheesecakes on a wire rack that's sitting on a parchment-lined baking sheet. Use an offset spatula or butter knife to carefully apply a thin layer of ganache to the tops and sides of each cutie. Let dry, then go over the cheesecakes again to smooth out any spots you may have missed, working from the top first and then down around the sides (dipping the spatula or knife in hot water and wiping dry periodically will also help keep the ganache smooth).

Garnish with sliced almonds and refrigerate 6 hours or overnight before serving. (You could chill the cuties overnight before adding ganache, then chill more briefly just to set the ganache. The cuties can be kept in the refrigerator for 3 days and are also freezable.)

My cuties: Victoria and Joseph

PBJ Wonder Cakewiches

page {66}

PB&J ALL GROWN-UP

Back in grade school, I yearned for peanut butter and jelly on squishy white Wonder bread. That's what all the other kids had, and who doesn't want to be like all the other kids? Instead, I always had something conspicuous and unmanageable, like leftover asparagus frittata on crusty Italian bread or salami and cheese but with a big slice of roasted eggplant on it that was impossible to bite through. Now that I'm all grownup it turns out I don't especially like the sandwich I thought I wanted—but I absolutely love using the elements in desserts. It's such fun to create a sophisticated take on the homey and humble components of something I once felt so deprived of. These PB&J–inspired desserts are kind of a double tribute—honoring the feelings I had as a child and celebrating the self-acceptance I found as an adult. As a kid, I thought I wanted to fit in. Now I know better, and these standout desserts celebrate that. Enjoy!

PB&J Wonder Cakewiches

Inspired by the humble lunchbox staple, these are absolutely adorable, extremely delicious, and certainly not just for kids. I recommend using unsweetened grape jelly because the tartness contrasts perfectly with the sweetness of the cake and the peanut butter buttercream (which is off-the-charts yummy and seriously addictive—I've been told it oughta be served with a warning label).

WONDER CAKE

1¾ cups cake flour

2 teaspoons baking powder

¼ teaspoon fine sea salt

4 ounces (1 stick) unsalted butter, softened

1 cup granulated sugar

½ cup whole milk, at room temperature

½ teaspoon vanilla

4 large egg whites, at room temperature

FILLING

½ cup Concord grape jelly, preferably all-fruit with no added sugar

1 cup Peanut Butter Buttercream (page 185), at room temperature

equipment

Two nonstick 12-cavity brownie pans (each cavity should be 2½ inches square)

Electric mixer

Preheat the oven to 350°F with a rack positioned in the center. Lightly grease the baking pans.

Sift together the flour, baking powder, and salt. Set aside.

Use a handheld electric mixer or stand mixer fitted with the paddle attachment to cream the butter until airy, 1 to 2 minutes. Gradually add the sugar and continue beating until fluffy and pale, 1 to 2 minutes more.

Add the flour mixture to the butter mixture in thirds, alternating with thirds of the milk and mixing just until smooth after each addition. Add the vanilla and mix briefly on low speed to combine.

In a clean, dry bowl beat the egg whites to stiff peaks.

Gently fold the egg whites into the batter. Divide the batter among the 24 square wells in the pans. Bake 8 to 10 minutes, or just until the centers spring back when gently pressed, rotating the pans halfway through the baking time. (You don't want to let the cakes brown much at all—only very slightly at the edges.)

Set the pans to cool on wire racks for 10 minutes before carefully turning out the cakes, then cool the cakes to room temperature. (The cakes can be made ahead, layered with parchment or wax paper in airtight containers or zip-top bags and refrigerated overnight or frozen. Thaw for 1 to 2 hours at room temperature before cutting and filling.)

Use a bread knife to cut the cakes in half to form 2 square layers (see photo on page 66). On the bottom halves spread a thin even layer of grape jelly, then spread on about ¼ inch of peanut butter buttercream. Top with the top halves and press gently with a flat spatula to affix securely. Chill 1 hour to set. Cut each chilled cake in half on the diagonal (to make 2 triangles). Let sit 15 minutes at room temperature before serving (to soften buttercream). The cakes can be kept covered and refrigerated for 2 to 3 days.

tip: Using pasteurized egg whites in both the cake and the buttercream saves time and doesn't leave you with lots of egg yolks (although you could use those for a curd or a custard. . .).

PB&J Baby Bundts

You will have a half cup or more of both drizzles left over after filling and decorating the PB&J Baby Bundts. Of course there are endless other uses—from froyo to French toast. You won't have any trouble finding enjoyable ways to dispose of the surplus. Both drizzles keep in the fridge for at least a week.

• MAKES 2 DOZEN •

PEANUT BUTTER CAKES

1¾ cups cake flour

2 teaspoons baking powder

¼ teaspoon fine sea salt

4 tablespoons (½ stick) butter, softened

1 cup granulated sugar

4 tablespoons creamy, unsweetened natural peanut butter

½ cup whole milk, at room temperature

½ teaspoon vanilla

4 large egg whites

FILLING

Raspberry Drizzle (page 182)

White Chocolate Drizzle (page 182)

equipment

Two heavyweight nonstick 12-cavity mini Bundt pans

Electric mixer

Preheat the oven to 350°F with racks positioned in the upper third and bottom third of the oven. Lightly grease the Bundt pans.

Sift together the flour, baking powder, and salt in a large bowl. Set aside.

Use a handheld electric mixer or stand mixer fitted with the paddle attachment to cream the butter until airy, 1 to 2 minutes. Gradually add the sugar and continue beating until fluffy and pale, 1 to 2 minutes more. Then gradually add the peanut butter, 1 tablespoon at a time, and beat another 1 to 2 minutes.

Add the flour mixture to the butter mixture in thirds, alternating with thirds of the milk and mixing just until smooth after each addition. Add the vanilla and mix briefly on low speed to combine.

In a clean, dry bowl beat the egg whites to stiff peaks.

Gently fold the egg whites into the batter.

Spoon 1 tablespoon of batter into each Bundt, spreading evenly. Top the center of each with 1 scant teaspoon of the raspberry filling followed by just enough batter to fill no more than two-thirds full (otherwise they will overflow during baking).

Bake 10 to 12 minutes, or until the tops of the cakes are evenly browned and spring back when gently pressed with a finger, rotating the pans front to back and top to bottom halfway through the baking time. Leave the cakes in the pans and cool to room temperature on wire racks.

Turn the cooled cakes out of the pans and set them on a baking sheet lined with parchment paper. Decorate with raspberry drizzle and white chocolate drizzle (I like to make lines of drizzle going down the ridges of the little cakes) and leave at room temperature (or refrigerate briefly) until the glaze is set. (Or cover and refrigerate up to 3 days. Bring to room temperature before serving.)

> tip: If you don't already own mini Bundt pans, they are definitely worth buying. It is so easy to use them for all sorts of recipes—cakes, breads, muffins, and even mousses. Just be sure to under- rather than overfill, especially the first time you are trying out a batter which you usually make in a regular pan. That way you will find out how much the batter rises in the small Bundt cavities without having an overflowed mess—or even cakes that have bulbous rather than flat bottoms.

Nutter Butter Finger Cakewiches

There is a certain packaged cookie that I have always loved, and there is a particular candy bar that I adore. One day I had a both on my mind and got to baking. This recipe is what happened. Crazy delicious!

• MAKES 4 DOZEN •

CAKE
1 recipe Peanut Butter Cake batter (page 68)

FILLING
1 cup Peanut Butter Buttercream (page 185),

½ cup finely chopped honey-roasted peanuts

Dark Chocolate Glaze (page 181)

equipment
Rimmed baking pan measuring 18 x 13 x 1 inches
Electric mixer

Preheat the oven to 350°F with a rack positioned in the center. Butter the rimmed baking pan then line with parchment, and butter and lightly flour the parchment, tapping out any excess flour.

Pour the batter into the prepared pan and bake just until springy in the center and barely beginning to brown at the edges (which will pull away from the pan), 10 to 15 minutes, rotating halfway through the baking time.

Set the buttercream out to soften while the cake bakes. Add the peanuts and mix thoroughly to combine.

Cool the cake in the pan on a wire rack for 5 minutes, then line the rack with parchment before turning out the cake so the wire won't cut into the surface. Let the cake cool completely before carefully peeling away the buttered parchment (set aside the parchment and baking sheet—you will use them again when you glaze the cake). (Cake can be double-wrapped and refrigerated overnight or frozen for 2 weeks. Thaw for 1 to 2 hours at room temperature before filling, glazing, and cutting.)

Transfer the cake to a flat work surface and use a large sharp knife and a ruler or other straight edge to cut in half crosswise. This will give you 2 rectangles, each roughly 8 by 12 inches.

Spread one half of the cake with the peanut butter buttercream. Carefully top with the other cake half. Chill for 30 minutes or until cream filling is firm. (Can be wrapped tightly in plastic and refrigerated overnight.)

To cut the cakes: Use a large sharp knife and a ruler or other straight edge to slice the cake crosswise into equal thirds. Then slice lengthwise into equal eighths. This will give you 24 little cakes, each about 1 inch wide and 2 inches long. Line up the cakes, spaced slightly apart, on the parchment and rimmed baking pan you used for baking.

Spoon chocolate glaze over each cake, covering the top and letting it drip down the sides.

Chill until glaze is set, about 2 hours (or overnight if covered).

Keep covered and refrigerated for up to 3 days. Set out at room temperature for 15 to 30 minutes before serving.

> tip: I always make the components for this recipe ahead. Then, the night before I'm planning to serve, I fill the cake and wrap it and leave it to set in the fridge overnight. The next morning, I cut and glaze the cakewiches and chill to set the glaze. I know from completing them days ahead that the glazed cakewiches keep well in the fridge for a few days, but I can't say there ever have been leftovers (when I make them ahead, I have to keep them in the basement fridge, unbeknownst to Rich and the kids!).

Hound Dogs

My mom and I love Elvis Presley—when I was growing up, we never missed any Elvis movies that played on Sunday afternoons. This rockin' dessert is inspired by the combo I've always heard he loved: peanut butter, bananas, and Fluff.

• MAKES 18 •

4 overripe bananas

½ cup packed light brown sugar

½ cup granulated sugar

4 ounces (1 stick) unsalted butter, at room temperature

2 large eggs, at room temperature

½ teaspoon vanilla extract

1½ cups all-purpose flour

½ teaspoon fine sea salt

FILLING
½ cup Peanut Butter Buttercream (page 185)

TOPPING
1 cup Marshmallow Cream (page 186)

equipment

Creme snack cake baking molds (aka cream canoes or Twinkie pans), with a total of 18 cavities and ⅓-cup capacity

Electric mixer with a whisk attachment

Two pastry bags with large star tips

Preheat the oven to 375°F. Grease the baking pans.

Peel the bananas and drop them into a large mixing bowl. Beat on high speed with an electric mixer fitted with a whisk attachment until light and creamy, 2 to 3 minutes.

Scrape down the sides of the bowl, add the sugars, and whip the mixture for 2 minutes.

Scrape down the sides of the bowl again, then add the butter and whip for another 2 minutes.

Scrape down the sides of the bowl once more and on medium speed beat in the eggs and the vanilla.

In a separate bowl, whisk together the flour and salt.

Add the dry ingredients to the wet ingredients and stir to combine. Do not overmix.

Drop about 3 tablespoons of the batter into each mold, filling each mold about halfway. Bake 15 to 20 minutes or until the tops are firm, springy, and lightly browned, rotating the pans halfway through the baking time. Set the pans on wire racks to cool completely to room temperature before turning out the cakes.

To fill the hound dogs, slice each cake in half lengthwise and use a piping bag fitted with a large star tip to pipe a thin layer of buttercream onto the bottom halves. Pipe a thin layer of marshmallow cream (not too much or it will overflow when you put the tops on). Replace the tops. Chill 15 to 30 minutes to set, then serve.

note: If you'd rather make these treats more conventional sandwich style, by all means go right ahead. Here's how: divide the batter between two 5¾-inch mini loaf pans; bake 45 to 50 minutes or until the tops are springy and a tester comes out clean; cool in the pans for about 15 minutes before turning out and setting on wire racks to cool to room temperature. Cut each loaf into about 12 slices, spread half of the slices with peanut butter buttercream and marshmallow cream, top each with another slice, and serve. Or just slice and let everyone make their own. Also, the banana bread recipe multiplies perfectly and freezes well, so there's no reason not to make extra.

*Chocolate
Babycakes*

page {76}

Chocolate—That's a Food Group, Right?

When Rosie and I were little, if we were well behaved in church—didn't laugh too much during prayer and hymns and got through the whole Mass without embarrassing my mother too much and having to be separated—then chances were good that along the walk back home Mom would stop at Cozy's Sweet Shop, just up the street from Saint James, and send us in with a quarter to buy a treat. This was a major highlight of my week. It was also a big dilemma: Almond Joy or Reese's? Red Twizzlers or the black licorice my mom liked? Starburst or Hot Tamales? It was so hard to choose! But I almost always ended up going for chocolate. Rosie, meanwhile, wasn't and still isn't into any kind of candy. She would have been fine with skipping the sweet shop and getting a calzone. I was the one with the crazy sweet tooth.

Obviously, I have never outgrown my sweet tooth. I still have a hard time choosing one dessert over another (that's why mini is the way to go—so you can have a little of this and a little of that, not just one big anything!). But when it comes down to it, the ultimate sweet for me is and will always be chocolate. There's just nothing like it—intoxicatingly rich, pure pleasure. It's a perfect base for mini desserts, because a small amount can deliver supreme satisfaction. And when it comes to romance, never ever underestimate the power of chocolate.

Chocolate Babycakes

These fudgy cakelets are very simple to make, but not to be rushed, and the details are important: eggs at room temperature, chocolate mixture cooled before adding, sifted cake flour, chocolate and then flour folded in by hand and not overmixed. As much room as there can be in baking for fun improvisation, this recipe is a good example of one of those times when rules need to be strict. Play by the rules on this one and you will have tender, moist cakes that are incredibly versatile—see the Chocolate-Tangerine Baby Bundts on page 78. Don't, and your cakes will be dry and heavy.

•MAKES 4 DOZEN•

BABYCAKES

4 ounces (1 stick) unsalted butter, cut into tablespoons

4 ounces unsweetened baking chocolate

4 eggs, at room temperature, separated

½ teaspoon fine sea salt

1 cup granulated sugar

1 teaspoon vanilla extract

1 cup cake flour (sifted then measured)

TOPPING

Chocolate Hazelnut Cream (page 184)

¼ cup toasted, chopped hazelnuts

¼ cup chocolate shavings

equipment

Electric mixer

Two heavyweight nonstick 24-cavity mini muffin pans

Pastry bag and large star tip

Preheat the oven to 350°F with a rack positioned in the center. Lightly grease the baking pan(s).

Combine the butter and the chocolate in a small heatproof bowl and set over a saucepan of barely simmering water. Cook, stirring frequently, until completely melted, thoroughly combined, and very smooth. Set aside to cool completely to room temperature.

In a large bowl combine the egg yolks and the salt and beat with an electric mixer at medium-high speed for 1 minute. Gradually add the sugar and continue beating at medium-high speed until fluffy. Mix in the vanilla. Use a flexible rubber spatula to gently fold in the cooled chocolate mixture by hand, mixing until not quite uniformly incorporated (it should still look swirly). Fold in the flour with as few strokes as possible, again mixing only until the batter is not quite uniformly colored.

In a clean dry bowl whip the egg whites to stiff peaks. Fold gently into the batter (it will become uniform in color but not in consistency, which will be lumpy—not to worry.)

Divide the batter among the mini muffin cups (about 1 tablespoon per cup).

Bake just until centers of the cakes are set, 8 to 10 minutes. Set the pan on a wire rack and let cool 5 to 10 minutes. (The cooled cakes can be wrapped and refrigerated for up to 3 days, or double-wrapped and frozen for up to 1 month.)

Line the wire rack with parchment and use a butter knife to gently turn the cakes out of the pans, setting the cakes upside down (narrower ends up—these will be the tops of the cakes; if the ends that will now be the bottoms have puffed you can trim them flat) and leaving to cool completely to room temperature.

To fill and top the cakes with hazelnut cream, fill a pastry bag fitted with a star tip halfway with the cream. Insert the tip into the flat top of each cake and pipe in cream, swirling as the cream begins to overflow to decorate the top of the cake. Add a sprinkling of hazelnuts and chocolate shavings to each cake

Chill the filled babycakes to set, about 1 hour. Let sit at room temperature 15 to 20 minutes before serving. (The cakes become firmer and brownie-like when they are refrigerated, so if you opt to make them ahead, be sure to bring them to room temperature if you want a lighter texture.)

Chocolate-Tangerine Baby Bundts

Rich, fudgy chocolate cake with a lavish layer of white chocolate that's spiked with the bright flavor of tangerine . . . pure magic. This recipe is an easy way to make that magic happen: prepare a variation on the batter for Chocolate Babycakes, switch the baking pan to a mini Bundt pan, layer the batter with citrusy white chocolate, and finish with tangerine-white chocolate drizzle.

•MAKES 1 DOZEN•

TANGERINE-WHITE CHOCOLATE DRIZZLE

1 small tangerine or clementine

2 tablespoons heavy cream

½ cup white chocolate chips

BABY BUNDTS

4 ounces (1 stick) unsalted butter, cut into tablespoons

4 ounces unsweetened baking chocolate

4 eggs, at room temperature, separated

½ teaspoon fine sea salt

1 cup granulated sugar

1 cup cake flour

TANGERINE-WHITE CHOCOLATE RIPPLE

1 small tangerine or clementine

½ cup white chocolate chips

equipment

Heavyweight nonstick 12-cavity mini Bundt pan

Microplane

Small squeeze bottle

Electric mixer

Preheat the oven to 350°F. Lightly coat the baking pan with non-stick cooking spray or vegetable oil from a misting bottle.

To make the drizzle, use a microplane to finely grate the zest from the tangerine. Transfer the zest to a small bowl. Squeeze the juice from the zested fruit into another small bowl. Add 1 tablespoon of the juice to the bowl with the zest. Reserve the remaining juice separately.

Combine the white chocolate and the cream in a small heatproof bowl and set over a small saucepan of barely simmering water. Heat, stirring occasionally, until completely melted and very smooth. Cool slightly, then stir in the reserved zest mixture. Transfer to a small squeeze bottle and set aside at room temperature.

To make the cake batter, in a small, heatproof bowl combine the butter and the chocolate and set over a saucepan of barely simmering water. Cook, stirring frequently, until completely melted, thoroughly combined, and very smooth. Cool completely to room temperature.

Combine the egg yolks and the salt in a large bowl and beat with an electric mixer at medium-high speed for 1 minute. Gradually add the granulated sugar and continue beating at medium-high speed until fluffy. Mix in the reserved tangerine juice.

Use a flexible rubber spatula to gently fold in the cooled chocolate mixture by hand, mixing until not quite uniformly incorporated (it should still look swirly). Fold in the flour with as few strokes as possible, again mixing only until the batter is not quite uniformly colored.

In a clean dry bowl whip the egg whites to stiff peaks. Fold gently into the batter (it will become uniform in color but not in consistency, which will be lumpy—not to worry).

To make the tangerine–white chocolate ripple, use the microplane to zest the tangerine; set aside the zest. Squeeze the zested tangerine into the bowl of reserved tangerine juice. Measure out 1 tablespoon of the juice and combine it in a small bowl with the zest and the white chocolate chips, stirring to coat the chips with the juice and zest. (If you have more juice left over, reserve for another use, or just knock it back—it's delish!).

Use a measuring spoon to scoop 1 tablespoon of the batter into each cavity in the baking pan. Top the center of each with 1 teaspoon of the white chocolate chip mixture. Cover the chips evenly with the remaining batter, filling each cavity no more than three-quarters of the way to the rim.

Bake about 15 minutes, or just until the tops of the cakes are puffed and dry. Leave the cakes in the pan and cool to room temperature on a wire rack. (The cooled cakes can be wrapped and refrigerated for up to 3 days, or double wrapped and frozen for up to 1 month.)

Turn the cooled cakes out of the pan and set them on a parchment-lined baking sheet. Decorate the tops of the Bundts with the drizzle (I like to make lines of drizzle down the sides of the Bundts, between the ridges). If the drizzle has thickened too much as it has cooled, stand the squeeze bottle in hot water for 1 to 2 minutes to soften to a squirtable consistency, then shake well before dispensing. Leave the drizzled cakes to set at room temperature for at least 1 hour before serving. (Or cover and refrigerate up to 3 days. Bring to room temperature before serving.)

> The cakes are best made a day or two ahead.

Chocolate Volcanoes

Look no further if a lavish dessert is what you're after. And romantic? These are intensely chocolatey, with oozing molten centers. Hello!

1 tablespoon butter, softened, for greasing ramekins

1 tablespoon unsweetened cocoa, for dusting ramekins

1 tablespoon granulated sugar, for dusting ramekins

2 large eggs

2 large egg yolks

¼ cup granulated sugar

1½ ounces bittersweet chocolate (60% cacao), chopped (¼ cup)

1½ ounces unsweetened baking chocolate, chopped (¼ cup)

4 tablespoons (½ stick) unsalted butter, cut into small pieces

2 tablespoons plus 2 teaspoons all-purpose flour

Confectioners' sugar, for dusting, optional

Raspberry Drizzle (page 182)

equipment

Six 3-ounce ramekins, or four 4-ounce ramekins

Stand mixer

Rimmed baking sheet

Preheat the oven to 425°F with a rack positioned in the center. Generously coat the ramekins with the softened butter. Whisk the cocoa and sugar together in a small bowl, then use the mixture to dust the ramekins, tapping out excess. Chill the ramekins while you prepare the batter.

Combine the eggs, yolks, and sugar in the bowl of a stand mixer fitted with the whisk and beat on medium-high until nearly tripled in volume and holds a ribbon when drizzled over itself, about 10 minutes.

Meanwhile, combine the chocolates and the butter in a small heatproof bowl set over a saucepan of barely simmering water. Cook, stirring frequently, until very smooth. Pour the hot chocolate mixture into the whipped egg mixture and fold gently until almost completely incorporated. Sprinkle the flour over the mixture and fold just until the flour is incorporated and the batter is uniformly blended.

Set the chilled prepared ramekins on a rimmed baking sheet. Divide the batter among the ramekins, filling almost to the top. (The unbaked cakes can be kept at room temperature for 1 to 2 hours; wrapped tightly in plastic and refrigerated for up to 2 days; or individually wrapped in plastic and frozen for 1 month.)

Bake just until the edges are set, about 6 minutes for 3-ounce, 8 minutes for 4-ounce; if frozen, add about 2 minutes.

Give the baked cakes 1 minute to settle. Then run the tip of a small sharp knife around the outer edge of each cake. Set a small plate serving-side down on top of each ramekin, then invert to unmold. Dust with confectioners' sugar, decorate with raspberry drizzle, and serve immediately.

> note: For a gluten-free version, replace the all-purpose flour with rice flour.

Nutty at Heart

Fudgy, brownie-like, heart-shaped cakes sandwiching lusciously peanut-buttery buttercream—what better way to say Happy Valentine's Day? Or Happy Any Day?

•MAKES 1 DOZEN•

CAKES

1 recipe Chocolate Babycakes batter (page 76)

FILLING

1 recipe Peanut Butter Buttercream (page 185),

½ cup finely chopped honey-roasted peanuts, divided

Chocolate shavings, for sprinkling

equipment

Twelve 2-inch, heart-shaped baking molds

Electric mixer

Pastry bag and large star tip

Preheat the oven to 350°F with a rack positioned in the center. Grease and lightly flour the baking molds, tapping out any excess flour.

Prepare the batter as instructed on page 76.

Set the molds on a baking sheet and divide the batter among the molds, filling each mold about halfway. Bake about 15 minutes, or just until the tops of the cakes are puffed and dry (not cracked). Transfer the baking sheet to a wire rack and let the cakes cool to room temperature. Carefully ease the cooled cakes out of the molds. (The cooled cakes can be wrapped and refrigerated for up to 3 days, or double wrapped and frozen for up to 1 month. Thaw for 1 to 2 hours at room temperature before cutting and filling.)

Transfer the cakes to a flat work surface and use a bread knife to slice each in half to create 2 heart-shaped layers.

Fold half of the honey-roasted peanuts into the peanut butter buttercream.

To fill the cakes with peanut butter buttercream, fill a pastry bag fitted with a star tip halfway with the frosting. Pipe the buttercream onto the bottom layer of each cake and top with the top layer. Pipe a star of buttercream on the top and sprinkle generously with chopped peanuts and chocolate shavings.

Chill to set, about 1 hour. Let sit at room temperature for 15 to 20 minutes before serving.

Coffee and Cake

Coffee was the very first thing I ever learned how to make all by myself in the kitchen, when I was seven or eight years old. Because I was a daddy's girl—adored and idolized him and was in awe of him—learning how to make coffee for him was a big deal for me. My dad was a man who always had to have coffee on demand. He and I were the two members of the family with a crazy sweet tooth; it was something special that we shared. Out of all my siblings, my brothers Ralph and Anthony share the Pierri sweet tooth as well, and they help critique my dessert recipes when I'm working on new ones, like for this book. Even if I don't get to deliver the treats myself, I'll send them home with my mom—since my brothers are always popping in on her I know I can count on getting their great feedback. You know how brothers are . . . brutally honest!! Just so you know, most of the recipes in this book have officially passed the brothers' test!

Turn the page for a great coffeecake recipe, one of my favorites that also happens to be one of Richie's favorites. I've made it for years now, and it's the perfect combination of all the things Daddy loved in sweets: fruit, nuts, and crumbly sugary streusel. (Technically, streusel is made with flour. Mine's not, but there's no better word for it than "streusel," so that's what I call it.)

Blueberry Streusel Baby Bundts

CAKE

1⅔ cups flour

¾ teaspoon baking powder

¾ teaspoon baking soda

½ teaspoon fine sea salt

4 ounces (1 stick) unsalted butter, at room temperature

½ cup granulated sugar

2 large eggs

1 teaspoon vanilla extract

1 cup sour cream

STREUSEL

½ cup light brown sugar

½ cup chopped walnuts

1 teaspoon cinnamon

1 cup fresh blueberries

equipment

Mini Bundt pan

Electric mixer

Pastry bag and large star tip

Preheat the oven to 375°F with two racks positioned in the upper and lower thirds of the oven. Lightly coat the baking pans with nonstick cooking spray or vegetable oil from an oil mister, then dust with flour, tapping out the excess.

In a large bowl, whisk together the flour, baking powder, baking soda, and salt. Set aside.

In a separate large bowl, use a mixer to cream the butter and sugar until light and fluffy. Add the eggs one at a time, beating well after each addition. Add the vanilla and blend, then add the flour mixture in thirds, alternating with the sour cream.

To make the streusel, stir together the brown sugar, walnuts, and cinnamon. Measure out and set aside ⅓ cup of the mixture. Toss the remaining streusel with the blueberries.

Divide ⅓ cup reserved streusel mixture among the wells of the Bundt pans (about ½ teaspoon each), then use a pastry bag to pipe in thin layers of the batter, alternating with layers of the blueberry mixture, filling each well no more than two-thirds full and finishing with a batter layer.

Bake 15 to 20 minutes, or until the tops of the cakes are evenly browned and spring back when gently pressed with a finger, rotating the pans halfway through the baking time.

Cool the cakes in the pans for 10 minutes before turning them out. Serve warm or at room temperature. (Can be double-wrapped and frozen for up to 3 months; thaw and gently reheat before serving.)

{spring}

My brother Anthony was born on Groundhog Day. Every year as we baked him a cake and sang him Happy Birthday, we were all anxiously wondering—given whatever prediction Punxsutawney Phil made that year—if we'd soon be celebrating the long-awaited spring or if we'd be stuck inside for a few more weeks of winter.

No sooner do the crocuses start peeking out through the snow than people seem to wake up to new possibilities, and that surge of energy and optimism increases as the trees begin to bud and a haze of green returns to the twigs that have been so brown and bare for so many months.

We know that we won't have to wait for spring's full bloom too much longer when Joseph's birthday comes along in March, and so does his saint's day—Saint Joseph's—which is a big celebration with many special foods (including Saint Joseph's zeppoli, which is filled with a crema similar to the one on page 90).

In this season of renewal, with everything coming back to life, traditional Italian desserts for this time of year center on a lot of eggs and dairy. With the solemnity of Lent and the celebration of Easter (one of my favorite holidays, such a beautiful time), spring is a time of reflection in the Church—a time for taking stock, resolving troubles, and coming together anew. It is a profound time that I find with each passing year becomes even more meaningful.

When I was a kid we often visited Italy at this time of year. My favorite day was the day after Easter, known as Pasquette (little Easter). Everyone would proudly pack up whatever they had baked and head from the farms up into the mountains and celebrate the firsts of spring and the beauty of God's gifts with a picnic.

Zia Regina's Flan

page {92}

La Crema

One of my most formative cooking memories is of helping my mother make custard cream. We got all the ingredients ready—eggs cracked and separated, cream and flour measured out, lemon juiced. Then we scooted my chair from the counter over to the stove and she had me climb back up because this time I got to work on the real cooking part. Ma stuck the handle of a regular dinner fork into the skin side of the juiced lemon half (I later learned this served two purposes: seasoning the crema with lemon essence and giving me more surface coverage while stirring). "Now stir, Kah-tee, stir," Mommy said, "and don't stop stirring or the crema, it will burn." She put the pan of cream and eggs over a low flame on the front burner and showed me how to stir the creamy mixture in wide circles and figure eights, making sure to keep moving it off the bottom of the pan so it wouldn't scorch. I stirred and stirred and stirred. Slowly, slowly the mixture got steamy and started to bubble gently. "Keep stirring! Keep stirring! Make sure you don't let it burn! As soon as it starts to get thick you tell me," Ma said. And I kept stirring, stirring, stirring, so nervous I would burn the custard and ruin everything, afraid that maybe I'd already blown it somehow because it seemed to me, with my little-kid sense of time and my tired little arm, that it was taking forever so something must be horribly wrong. But then the magical moment came, and my fork was moving through a beautiful silky custard. Something so extraordinary from a few simple ingredients, the right heat level over the right length of time, plus proper measures of elbow grease and patience. I was amazed by the transformation and thrilled to discover I could have a creative role. It was a wonderful gift, to learn at such a young age that I had the ability to change the properties of things by being a part of the equation—like an alchemist.

Nonni Maria's Custard Cream

This is a *crema* that my mother, Maria Domenica Gorga Pierri, learned to make from Zia Rosa, the aunt who raised her in the town of Sala Consilina in the province of Salerno in the Campania region of southern Italy. Mom remembers Zia Rosa making this cream often and using it to fill small rounds of fried dough whenever they wanted something sweet and special. There was another *zia* who used the same cream to fill cannoli. On its own, *crema* is a lovely Old World dessert, sweet and creamy, simple but sumptuous—pudding, basically, and who doesn't love vanilla pudding? Whether you serve the custard in little glasses or bowls, warm (as a pouring custard) or chilled, with or without fresh fruit or a warm fruit compote (like stewed rhubarb or poached pears), or you layer it into parfaits, fill a cake with it (like my mom did when I was growing up—yum!), or use it as pastry cream in a tart shell topped with fruit—the possibilities are endless and you truly cannot go wrong.

• MAKES 8 TO 10 •

2 cups whole milk, divided

½ cup granulated sugar, divided

3 large egg yolks

3 tablespoons cornstarch

2 tablespoons lemon juice

3 tablespoons unsalted butter, cut into tablespoons and softened

equipment

Fine-mesh sieve

Eight to ten 2- to 3-ounce dessert bowls, ramekins, or glasses

Combine 1 cup of the milk and ¼ cup of the sugar in a medium saucepan. Bring the mixture to a boil over medium heat and immediately remove the pan from the heat and pour the mixture into a large measuring cup with a spout.

In a medium bowl lightly beat the egg yolks, then whisk in the remaining ¼ cup sugar, the remaining 1 cup milk, and the cornstarch, mixing until very smooth (put the mixture through a wire sieve if any lumps of cornstarch persist).

Pour the scalded milk in a slow thin stream into the egg mixture, whisking constantly. Pour the entire mixture back into the saucepan and bring it to a boil over medium-low heat, whisking constantly, until thick and creamy, about 5 minutes.

Take the pan off the heat and stir in the lemon juice and the butter, mixing until smooth and thoroughly incorporated.

Serve warm as a pouring custard, or divide among 10 to 12 small dessert bowls or glasses and chill thoroughly, covered with plastic wrap lightly pressed onto the surface of the custard to prevent a skin from forming. Chill 2 hours or overnight before serving. Can be made up to 4 days ahead.

tip: To make chocolate custard cream, replace the lemon juice with 1 teaspoon of vanilla extract. Once you've stirred in the butter, pour the hot custard over 8 ounces of finely chopped semisweet chocolate. Let set 2 minutes, then stir until smooth and blended.

Zia Regina's Flan

My father's sister Regina emigrated from Italy to Brazil in the 1940s. My dad and she were close in age and adored each other. They also are the two siblings who looked most alike, so it is especially moving to see her every time she comes to America to visit. Zia Regina is a very stylish lady with flamboyant charm, a touch of Brazilian spice mixed in with her Italian brio. She taught my mom and me how to make flan the traditional way it is served in Brazil. *Delicioso!*

· MAKES 1 DOZEN ·

1¼ cups granulated sugar

One 14-ounce can sweetened condensed milk

1¾ cups whole milk

3 large eggs

equipment

Blender

Twelve 4-ounce ramekins

Heat the sugar in a medium saucepan over medium-high heat until the sugar melts and darkens to an amber brown color, about 5 minutes, swirling occasionally to dissolve all of the sugar and distribute the color uniformly.

Working quickly and carefully (and gently rewarming the caramel if it cools and begins to solidify), use a metal tablespoon to divide the caramelized sugar among the baking dishes, tilting each dish to coat the bottom (don't worry if you don't get it to spread much). Set the dishes aside and allow the caramelized sugar to cool and harden completely.

Preheat the oven to 350°F with a rack positioned in the center.

Combine the milks and eggs in a blender and whip for 1 minute. Divide the milk mixture among the baking dishes, and set the dishes in a roasting pan or other large rimmed baking dish. Add hot water to the roasting pan to fill at least halfway up the sides of the dishes. Bake until the tops of the flans are lightly golden and a toothpick inserted into the center comes out clean, 30 to 35 minutes (the flan will appear to be a bit wobbly but will firm up as it cools).

Cool to room temperature, then chill in the refrigerator for at least 6 hours before serving. Once the flan is completely chilled, run the tip of a sharp knife around the edge of each baking dish, then set a dessert plate (one large enough to fit the flan as well as the caramel syrup) on top of each baking dish and invert to unmold, with the caramel pooling around the custard.

Strawberry Panna Cotta

Victoria adores fruit desserts, especially strawberry ones, so in the springtime I love to dress up panna cotta ("cooked cream") with the first early local strawberries of the season, incorporating them into the cream itself and topping each serving with a little strawberry-and-herb coulis. You need to allow plenty of chilling time (which makes it a perfect make-ahead dessert), but the time it takes to prepare is minimal—10 to 15 minutes, tops. These are lovely unmolded onto dessert plates and garnished with the bright red and green topping, but if you are making them for a big do and know you need to keep things simple at serving time, chill in small glasses and skip the unmolding step.

•MAKES 1 DOZEN•

PANNA COTTA

16 ounces fresh strawberries, hulled and sliced (3 cups)

1 cup low-fat buttermilk

½ cup granulated sugar

¼ cup cold water

2¼ teaspoons (1 packet) unflavored gelatin

2 cups heavy cream

1 teaspoon vanilla extract

STRAWBERRY TOPPING

16 ounces fresh strawberries, hulled and diced (3 cups)

6 tablespoons granulated sugar

1½ tablespoons freshly squeezed lemon juice

3 tablespoons chopped fresh mint or basil

equipment

Blender

Twelve 3-ounce ramekins, molds, or glasses

To make the panna cotta, combine the strawberries, buttermilk, and sugar in a blender and purée until smooth. Use a large spoon to press the mixture through a fine-mesh sieve into a medium bowl. Set aside the strained purée (discard solids from the sieve).

Pour the cold water into a small bowl and sprinkle the gelatin over the surface. Let sit for about 1 minute for the gelatin to soften.

In a small saucepan heat the remaining heavy cream over medium heat until it comes to a boil, then immediately remove the saucepan from the heat, add the gelatin mixture to the cream, and whisk until the gelatin is dissolved and the mixture is smooth.

Whisk the cream mixture into the strawberry purée. Mix in the vanilla. Pour the panna cotta into small custard cups, molds, or flutes. Cover tightly with plastic wrap and chill until firm, at least 5 hours. (Can be made up to 2 days ahead.)

To make the coulis, combine the diced strawberries, sugar, lemon juice, and herbs. Toss gently to mix, then set aside to macerate at room temperature for 30 minutes.

To unmold, dip the bottom of each dish into a small bowl of hot water to help loosen, then run a sharp knife around the edge and invert onto a dessert plate. Top with strawberry coulis immediately before serving.

Chocolate Custard Tartlets

Growing up, Stella D'oro Swiss Fudge was my absolute favorite store-bought cookie. That is definitely the inspiration here, but in my rendition the little star-shaped treats become tartlets, with a thin and delicate shell and silky chocolate custard filling.

• MAKES 4 DOZEN •

SHORTBREAD PASTRY

8 ounces (2 sticks) unsalted butter, at room temperature

¾ cup granulated sugar

2 teaspoons vanilla extract

2 cups all-purpose flour

¼ teaspoon fine sea salt

All-purpose flour, for dusting

CHOCOLATE CUSTARD FILLING

8 ounces semisweet chocolate

Nonni Maria's Custard Cream (page 90), lemon juice omitted, kept warm

1 teaspoon vanilla extract

equipment

Two heavyweight nonstick 24-cavity mini muffin pans

Electric mixer

2½-inch round cutter, or a glass, can, or bowl with an opening of that diameter

Small pastry tamper, optional

Two large rimmed baking sheets

To make the pastry shells, cream together the butter and sugar in a large bowl. Mix in the vanilla.

In a separate small bowl, sift together the flour and salt.

With the mixer at low speed, slowly add the flour mixture to the butter mixture and continue mixing at low speed just until it looks pebbly, frequently scraping down the sides of the bowl.

Gently pat the pebbly bits together into a dough, then turn the dough out onto a work surface lined with a sheet of parchment, wax paper, or plastic wrap. Form the dough into a ball, flatten into a disk, then wrap tightly and chill in the refrigerator for 1 hour or up to 3 days (or freeze for up to 3 months).

Lightly flour the dough on both sides and roll it out between two sheets of lightly floured parchment paper to an even thickness of ⅛ inch. Use a 2½-inch cutter to cut 48 circles, rerolling scraps as needed. (The dough will be a bit crumbly; if it breaks apart just stick it back together, it mends easily.)

Thoroughly coat the muffin pans with nonstick spray or vegetable oil from a mister.

Carefully transfer the dough circles to the pans, using a pastry tamper or your fingers to press into place (again, mend as needed). Set the pans on baking sheets and transfer to the refrigerator to chill for 1 hour.

Preheat the oven to 350°F with a rack positioned in the center. Bake the pastry shells (on the baking sheets) until lightly golden, about

10 minutes. If the bottoms of the shells have puffed up, lightly press them down with the tamper to flatten. Set the sheets on wire racks and leave the shells to cool all the way to room temperature.

To make the filling, finely chop the chocolate and transfer it to a medium bowl. Set aside.

Prepare the custard according to the instructions on page 90, omitting the lemon juice and adding the vanilla.

Pour the hot custard over the chopped chocolate and let sit 2 minutes, then stir until smooth and blended.

Transfer the custard to a large measuring cup with a spout. Cool to room temperature. (If it cools too much, it will set—no worries: use a mini scoop to put the custard in the shells.) Fill the cooled pastry shells, then chill until firm (covered with plastic wrap lightly pressed into surface of pudding). Or serve warm, à la *pot de crème*.

> *shortcut*: Use premade mini tart shells or pastry cups.

The Choux Maker's Daughter

Don't get me wrong, I love cupcakes, but enough is enough already, right? Same goes for macaroons, whoopie pies, and artisanal donuts, the other retro desserts that have been all the rage lately. *Basta!* Of course, hopeless sweet tooth that I am, I love them all. But the old-fashioned dessert that gets my vote for a big comeback is the cream puff. Cream puffs are classic, they are both elegant and adorable, they are uniquely delectable (airy *and* creamy!), and they are endlessly versatile. Plus the little puff shells (choux) freeze beautifully, so you can bust them out just about any time, no sweat. Maybe best of all: they seem difficult to make but really and truly are not. You can also fill the choux with ice cream and call them profiteroles. Or pipe in short strips rather than mounds, bake, halve, fill with pastry cream (*La Crema*, page 90), and glaze with chocolate (page 181), and *voilà*: eclairs!

Pulcinelli Limoni

Little Lemon Chicks

Whenever I make a batch of these adorable little puffs with bright yellow filling peeking out, I'm reminded of the fluffy yellow chicks we'd see at the pet store next to my dad's shoe repair shop when I was little.

LEMON CREAM FILLING

½ cup cold heavy whipping cream

1 recipe cold Lemon Curd (page 183)

SHELLS

6 tablespoons water

6 tablespoons whole milk

6 tablespoons unsalted butter, diced

¼ teaspoon fine sea salt

¾ cup sifted all-purpose flour

3 large eggs

Confectioners' sugar, for serving

Long, thin strips of lemon zest, for serving

equipment

Stand mixer

Two large baking sheets

Zester

Pastry bag and large round tip

To make the lemon cream filling, whip the cream to stiff peaks, then fold it into the lemon curd. Cover and chill for up to 2 days.

To make the choux, preheat the oven to 425°F with one rack positioned in the top third of the oven and one rack positioned in the bottom third. Line 2 large baking sheets with parchment paper.

Combine the water, milk, butter, and salt in a heavy-bottom saucepan over medium heat. Once the butter is melted, add the flour all at once and stir vigorously until a dough forms and pulls away from the sides of the saucepan, 1 to 2 minutes. Continue turning the dough 1 to 2 more minutes (it will form a ball), then remove the saucepan from the heat.

Transfer the dough to the bowl of a stand mixer and let it cool for 5 minutes. Put the paddle attachment on the mixer, turn on the machine to medium-low, and add the eggs 1 at a time, blending in each egg before adding the next. Continue beating the dough until it is smooth and shiny, 2 to 3 minutes.

Working in batches, transfer the dough to a large pastry bag fitted with a ½-inch plain round tip and pipe 1-inch rounds, spacing them 2 inches apart, onto the prepared baking sheets. Smooth the tops with a wet finger. You can also scoop rounded tablespoons of the dough onto the baking sheets, but piping is much neater. (You can freeze the unbaked dough on the baking sheets, then transfer to freezer bags. Bake without thawing, adding a couple of minutes to the baking time.)

Bake the puffs for 15 minutes at 425°F. Then quickly rotate the baking sheets top to bottom and front to back, and lower the oven temperature to 350°F. Continue baking just until the puffs are dry, firm, and golden brown, about 10 more minutes, keeping a very close eye on them to prevent overbrowning. Cool the puffs on baking sheets. Do not fill until completely cooled to room temperature. (The baked, cooled, unfilled puffs can be frozen for up to 3 months. Freeze on the baking trays, transferring to zip-top freezer bags once frozen. Thaw at room temperature before filling.)

To fill the puffs, use a small sharp knife to cut the top quarter off of each puff. Pull out any soft dough that remains in the bottoms of the puffs, and use a pastry bag fitted with ½-inch star tip to pipe lemon cream into the shells. You can also use a small spoon to fill the puffs, but piping is much neater and also makes for airier filling. Top each puff with its cut-off top (like a little hat).

Dust the puffs with confectioners' sugar, garnish with curls of lemon zest, and serve.

Strawberry Shortcake Puffs

Swap in choux for shortcake, fill with strawberry cream instead of plain whipped cream, and finish with a simple strawberry sauce—every bit as sweet and comforting as the all-American original, but with the airy magic of a cream puff.

•MAKES ABOUT 4 DOZEN•

12 ounces fresh strawberries, hulled, or one 12-ounce bag frozen strawberries, thawed

2 tablespoons Chambord or other berry liqueur

½ cup granulated sugar

1½ teaspoons cornstarch

1 cup cold heavy cream

4 dozen cream puff shells (page 98)

Chantilly cream (page 183), for serving

Sliced fresh strawberries, for garnish

equipment

Food processor

Stand mixer

Combine the strawberries, liqueur, and sugar in a medium bowl, stir to mix, then leave to macerate at room temperature for about 30 minutes.

Transfer the soaked fruit to the bowl of a food processor fitted with a standard blade and process it to a fine purée.

Scoop ¼ cup of the purée into a small bowl; cover and refrigerate until well chilled.

To make the strawberry drizzle, transfer the remaining strawberry purée to a small saucepan and bring it to a gentle simmer over medium-low heat. Simmer 5 minutes, then press the fruit through a fine-mesh sieve set over a small bowl, pressing with a spoon. Scrape into the bowl any fruit mixture that clings to the outside of the sieve. Discard the solids trapped in the sieve and transfer the strained mixture back to the saucepan. In a small bowl combine the cornstarch with 1 teaspoon water and stir until completely dissolved and very smooth. Add the slurry to the pan and stir the mixture constantly until it thickens, about 3 minutes. Remove from the heat, cool to room temperature, and transfer to a squeeze bottle or pitcher.

To make the strawberry cream, in a stand mixer fitted with a whisk, whip the cold cream to very stiff peaks. Gradually add the chilled berry purée and whip until well combined. Cover with plastic wrap and refrigerate until ready to use; rewhip if needed before spooning into cream puffs.

Make the cream puff shells, baking and cooling them, then cutting off the tops as directed on page 98. Spoon chilled strawberry cream into the puffs. Top each with a small dollop of Chantilly cream and a zigzag of strawberry drizzle. Garnish with sliced fresh strawberries.

Chocolate Hazelnut Kisses

I wanted to make a cream puff that says "I love you" like a Baci candy (chocolate-hazelnut truffle filling mixed with chopped hazelnuts, topped with a whole hazelnut, and covered in dark chocolate—OMG). Mission accomplished!

•MAKES ABOUT 4 DOZEN•

5 tablespoons Nutella chocolate hazelnut spread

3 tablespoons semisweet chocolate chips

6 tablespoons cold heavy cream

4 dozen cream puff shells (page 98)

Cocoa powder, for serving

Toasted chopped hazelnuts, for serving

Chocolate shavings, for serving

equipment

Electric mixer

Pastry bag and large round tip

Combine the Nutella and the chocolate in a medium heatproof bowl and set over a small saucepan of barely simmering water. Cook for about 5 minutes or until the ingredients are completely melted and incorporated, stirring almost constantly with a whisk or a heatproof flexible spatula and frequently scraping down the sides of the bowl. The mixture will be very smooth and silky. Set aside to cool to room temperature, 20 to 30 minutes.

In a large bowl whip the cream to stiff peaks with an electric mixer. Add the cooled chocolate mixture and whip with the mixer until well combined. Cover with plastic wrap and refrigerate until ready to use. Soften at room temperature for 15 to 20 minutes before piping or spooning.

Make the cream puff shells, baking and cooling them, then cutting off the tops as directed on pages 98. Pipe or spoon chilled chocolate hazelnut filling into the puffs (piping is much neater and also makes for airier filling). Dust the serving dish(es) with cocoa powder, top with cream puff(s), and sprinkle the puffs with toasted hazelnuts and chocolate shavings.

Bananas Foster Cream Puff Cuties

These caramel banana cream-filled delights are reminiscent of the classic New Orleans dessert. Yes, there is a little rum involved (the darker the better!), but, unlike the original, no flambéing.

2 ripe bananas, peeled

1 teaspoon cinnamon

¼ cup packed dark brown sugar

2 teaspoons dark rum

1 tablespoon butter

1 cup cold heavy whipping cream

1 teaspoon vanilla extract

4 dozen cream puff shells (page 98)

Caramel Drizzle (page 180), for serving

Toasted chopped pecans, for serving

equipment

Electric mixer

Pastry bag and large round tip

Mash the bananas together with the cinnamon, brown sugar, and rum, using a fork to thoroughly combine. Melt the butter in a skillet over medium heat and add the banana mixture. Cook, stirring constantly, for 3 to 5 minutes, until the mixture is fragrant and the liquid has evaporated. Let the mixture cool to room temperature. Cover and chill.

Make the cream puff shells, baking and cooling them, then cutting off the tops as directed on pages 98–99.

Whip the cream and the vanilla to stiff peaks. Fold in the cold banana mixture in thirds.

Pipe or spoon the banana filling into the cream puff shells (piping is much neater and also makes for airier filling). Serve with caramel drizzle and toasted chopped pecans.

Love Nests

Shredded phyllo dough (*knafeh* or *kataifi*)—basically the same delicately layered pastry as regular phyllo but in thin papery vermicelli-like strands—is the base for many crunchy sticky desserts across the eastern Mediterranean and the Middle East. One of the various ways *knafeh* is traditionally used in Lebanon is layered with fresh cheese and bathed in sugar syrup. Whenever Richie's mom makes her *knafeh*, it's a big deal, a real showstopper at family gatherings. People exclaim, "Wow! Homemade *knafeh*!" It is truly amazing, with creamy cheese, luscious syrup called *attar* that's so thick it's almost velvety, and the crisp, flaky phyllo shreds grabbing up the syrup.

Instead of making it in big trays and cutting it into pieces, I like to form the *knafeh* into little birds' nests. In the following pages you'll find Basic Birds' Nests, with the traditional elements. Then there are two renditions that have very personal inspirations behind them: blue jays (because there was one that visited me daily just after my father passed away), and cardinals (because I felt my father-in-law's presence in the days after he died whenever I saw one of these beautiful red birds that he'd always loved). And my Doves' Nests I created with prayers for peace very much in my mind and heart, amid these times of so much conflict around the world and too often in our personal lives as well.

Knafeh Nests

Frozen shredded phyllo can be found in the freezer case of most Middle Eastern and Mediterranean food markets (it is usually labeled *knafeh* or *kataifi*). It will dry out very quickly if not properly handled and stored (see the instructions in the recipe that follows). Brushing shredded phyllo with melted butter before baking helps to prevent sticking and cracking and results in a beautiful golden color after baking.

If you can get to a good Middle Eastern market, you can use ackawi cheese, a firm white cheese curd that is more or less the same as what's used to make fresh mozzarella. You can also substitute fresh mozzarella (slice it, soak in water, and rinse to remove some of the salt).

Any leftover syrup can be used to sweeten cocktails or tea.

• MAKES 2 DOZEN •

4 ounces (1 stick) unsalted butter

¼ pound (¼ package) shredded phyllo dough (usually labeled *kataifi* or *knafeh*), defrosted overnight in the refrigerator then brought to room temperature

1½ cups coarsely grated or shredded mozzarella curd, best slightly frozen or stored in freezer for an hour before grating

½ cup whole-milk ricotta

Orange Blossom Syrup (page 179), to serve

equipment

Heavyweight nonstick 24-cavity mini muffin pan

To clarify the butter, slowly melt it in a heavy-bottom saucepan over low heat. After about 5 minutes it will begin to bubble and foam. Take the pan off the heat and let the butter settle for 3 to 5 minutes. The milky solids will sink to the bottom of the pan. Carefully pour off the clear liquid into a container, leaving the solids behind (discard the solids). (The clarified butter can be made ahead; it will keep in an airtight container in the refrigerator for months.)

Preheat the oven to 350°F with a rack positioned in the center. Lightly brush the mini muffin pans with clarified butter.

Separate the shredded lengths of phyllo into ¼-inch thick bundles. (Keep the portion you are not working with covered with a sheet of plastic wrap topped with a clean and very slightly dampened dish towel to keep it from drying out.) Working in small batches, brush the strands lightly with butter and place enough phyllo in each well of the pan to cover so none of the pan shows through, molding the strands into little nests (don't worry about them being perfect, rustic is part of their charm). Repeat this process until all of the wells in the pan are filled. Drizzle the remaining butter over the nests and use a brush to dab the butter so that it soaks into the phyllo threads a bit.

In a mixing bowl combine the mozzarella curd and the ricotta, stirring until evenly mixed. Drop a rounded teaspoonful of the cheese mixture into each nest and smooth over to make a small mound. Distribute any remaining cheese mixture over each nest.

Bake for 15 minutes until the edges of the phyllo are lightly golden brown. (Nests can be made ahead and kept covered with plastic wrap in refrigerator for 1 day or frozen for about 2 weeks. Rewarm briefly in oven or toaster oven.)

Serve warm, with orange blossom syrup in a little pitcher for everyone to drizzle on to taste.

> tip: Use a large knife to cut off ¼ of the frozen *knafeh*, rewrap both pieces so that the ¼ can be thawed and the rest can go back in the freezer. Alternatively, thawed shredded phyllo can be stored for about 1 week in the refrigerator wrapped tightly in plastic wrap under a damp towel.

Doves' Nests

I love how the aromatic cinnamon and star anise, along with the zesty ginger and sweet-tart orange juice, perk up the mellow richness of the apricots and almonds in this filling.

•MAKES 2 DOZEN•

Knafeh Nests (page 106), baked but syrup not poured on

APRICOT–ALMOND FILLING

1 cup diced dried apricots

1 tablespoon diced crystallized ginger

½ cup orange juice

1 cinnamon stick

2 star anise

2 tablespoons Amaretto

¼ cup slivered toasted almonds

Orange Blossom Syrup (page 179), to serve

To make the filling, combine the apricots, ginger, orange juice, cinnamon stick, star anise, and Amaretto in a medium heavy-bottom saucepan over medium-low heat. Simmer for a few minutes, just until apricots are softened and all liquid is dissolved. Allow to cool to room temperature.

Fill each nest with a teaspoon of apricot filling and garnish with a sprinkling of toasted almonds. (Nests can be made ahead and kept covered with plastic wrap in the refrigerator for 1 day or frozen for about 2 weeks. Rewarm briefly in oven or toaster oven.)

Serve warm, with orange blossom syrup in a little pitcher for everyone to drizzle on to taste.

Blue Jays' Nests

I always say that we savor food first with our eyes. That definitely holds true for this dessert, with its combination of blueberries and pine nuts that is as luscious to behold as it is to nibble.

Knafeh Nests (page 106), baked but syrup not poured on

BLUEBERRY–PINE NUT FILLING

2 cups fresh blueberries

⅓ cup granulated sugar

3 tablespoons Chambord or blueberry liqueur

¼ cup lightly toasted pine nuts

Orange Blossom Syrup (page 179), to serve

equipment

Blender

To make the filling, combine the blueberries, sugar, and liqueur in a medium heavy-bottom saucepan. Bring to a boil over medium-high heat and cook for a few minutes, just until the blueberries start to soften and release their juices. Then lower the heat and simmer until the liquid begins to thicken, 7 to 10 minutes.

Let the filling cool slightly, then use a blender or food processor to purée finely. Cool completely to room temperature, then spoon about ½ teaspoon into each nest. (Nests can be made ahead and kept covered with plastic wrap in the refrigerator for 1 day or frozen for about 2 weeks. Rewarm briefly in oven or toaster oven.)

Serve warm, with orange blossom syrup in a little pitcher for everyone to drizzle on to taste.

Cardinals' Nests

Cherries, pistachios, and pomegranates are all ingredients that I associate with ancient Mediterranean cultures—a fitting tribute for my father-in-law, Joseph Wakile, whom we all miss so dearly.

•MAKES 2 DOZEN•

Knafeh Nests (page 106), baked but syrup not poured on

CHERRY-PISTACHIO FILLING

1 cup chopped dried cherries

3 tablespoons cherry liqueur, or Chambord or another cherry- or berry-flavored liqueur

¼ cup mini semisweet chocolate chips

1 tablespoon heavy cream

¼ cup finely chopped pistachios

¼ cup pomegranate seeds

Orange Blossom Syrup (page 179), to serve

To make the filling, combine the cherries, Chambord, and ¼ cup water in a medium heavy-bottom saucepan and simmer a few minutes until the cherries soften and liquid is absorbed. Remove from heat and set aside to cool to room temperature.

Combine the chocolate chips and heavy cream in a small microwave safe bowl and microwave for approximately 30 seconds to melt the chocolate. Stir until smooth.

Top each nest with a small dollop of chocolate followed by about ½ teaspoon of cherry filling. Garnish with a sprinkling of chopped pistachios and pomegranate seeds. (Nests can be made ahead and kept covered with plastic wrap in refrigerator for 1 day or frozen for about 2 weeks. Rewarm briefly in oven or toaster oven.)

Serve warm, with orange blossom syrup in a little pitcher for everyone to drizzle on to taste.

My father, Anthony Pierri, Victoria, and my father-in-law, Joseph Wakile

. . . And *Who* Has More Fun?

You'd never know it to look at me now, but I started out life as a true blonde. For real! But not a head of all-American-as-apple-pie, Barbie-straight gleaming locks (and not the fair skin and twinkly little eyes to match). Nope: I had wildly wavy blond hair. And dark, bronze skin. And, yes, blue eyes, but huge round blue ones. Eventually my other features caught up—well almost. The eyes are still pretty big. It took a long time before I grew out of wishing I looked like Farrah Fawcett or Cheryl Tiegs (with a little help from smokin' hot brunette powerhouses on TV, like Wonder Woman, Veronica, the wicked twin sister on *Bewitched,* and the troublemaking sister on *I Dream of Jeannie*) and came to appreciate and embrace my exotic Italian looks.

So when it comes to blondies and brownies, I like to have some fun either way. All are bite-size, of course, baked in mini muffin pans and inverted to serve flat tops up (whether drizzled or not, the somewhat pyramidal shape has a certain charm all its own—and means no one mistakes them for muffins, ever). There's white chocolate in my basic blondie, to give it a little chewy oomph. And I go very tropical with the Beach Baby Blondies. Bitsy Brunettes are a classic walnut brownie, while the chili-chocolate variation is something else altogether.

White Chocolate Blondie Bites

Cute as little bitty buttons with their stripes of white chocolate drizzle, these are a great, easy, make-ahead treat—actually best made at least 1 day before serving and kept at room temperature, taking on a caramelly chewiness over time. And they freeze beautifully!

1 cup all-purpose flour

½ teaspoon baking powder

⅛ teaspoon fine sea salt

4 ounces (1 stick) unsalted butter, melted

½ cup packed dark brown sugar

1 cup white chocolate chips

1 large egg

1½ teaspoons vanilla extract

White Chocolate Drizzle (page 182)

equipment

Heavyweight nonstick 24-cavity mini muffin pan

Preheat the oven to 350°F and position a rack in the center.

Sift the flour, baking powder, and salt together into a small bowl and set aside.

Combine the melted butter and sugar in a large bowl and whisk together until smooth and creamy.

Melt the white chocolate in a heatproof bowl over a small saucepan of barely simmering water, stirring occasionally, until very smooth.

Add the white chocolate to the butter mixture, whisking until smooth and well blended. Then whisk in the egg and vanilla followed by the flour mixture.

Scoop the batter into the muffin pan, dividing evenly among the 24 cups.

Bake 8 minutes, or just until the edges are golden brown and a tester comes out clean (the blondies will be very soft). Set the pan on a wire rack and let cool all the way to room temperature (they may sink in the centers—not to worry), then use a butter knife to ease each blondie out.

Transfer the blondies to a plate or work surface lined with parchment or wax paper. Flip them over (flat bottoms facing up) and decorate with white chocolate drizzle, using a zigzag motion to create a pretty pattern. Let sit or refrigerate to set. Best made 1 day ahead; can be stored in an airtight container at room temperature for about a week.

Beach Baby Blondies

Rich macadamia nuts and coconut, sweet chewy dried pineapple, and zingy lime give these a scrumptiously tropical twist. As with the basic blondies, they are best served the day after they're baked. They freeze extremely well.

•MAKES 2 DOZEN•

1 cup all-purpose flour

½ teaspoon baking powder

Pinch salt, optional

4 ounces (1 stick) unsalted butter, melted

½ cup packed dark brown sugar

1 cup white chocolate chips

1 large egg

1½ teaspoons vanilla extract

½ cup coarsely chopped dried sweetened pineapple

¼ cup roasted salted macadamia nuts, coarsely chopped

¼ cup unsweetened grated coconut

Lime–White Chocolate Drizzle (page 115)

equipment

Heavyweight nonstick 24-cavity mini muffin pan

Preheat the oven to 350°F with a rack positioned in the center.

Sift together the flour, baking powder, and salt in a small bowl and set aside.

Combine the melted butter and sugar in a large bowl and whisk together until smooth and creamy.

Melt the white chocolate in a heatproof bowl over a small saucepan of barely simmering water, stirring occasionally, until very smooth. Add the white chocolate to the butter mixture, whisking until smooth and well blended. Then whisk in the egg and the vanilla.

Add the flour mixture, stirring well to combine, then add the pineapple, macadamia nuts, and coconut.

Scoop the batter into the prepared muffin pan, dividing evenly among the 24 cups.

Bake 8 minutes, or just until the edges are golden brown and a tester comes out clean (the blondies will be very soft). Set the pan on a wire rack and let cool to room temperature, then use a butter knife to ease each blondie out.

Transfer the blondies to a plate or work surface lined with parchment or wax paper. Flip them over (flat bottoms facing up) and decorate with lime–white chocolate drizzle, using a zigzag motion to create a nice striping pattern. Let sit or refrigerate to set. Best made 1 day ahead; can be kept in an airtight container at room temperature for about a week.

note: If your macadamia nuts are heavily salted, you might want to make the pinch of salt a small one, or omit it altogether. Taste the macadamias before you decide—a distinct saltiness is one of the elements that makes these blondies amazing. You just don't want to let it overwhelm the other flavors.

Lime–White Chocolate Drizzle *Makes about ¾ cup*

1 lime

¾ cup white chocolate chips

¼ cup heavy cream

equipment

Microplane

Squeeze bottle

Use a microplane to finely grate the zest from the lime into a small bowl. Squeeze the lime juice into the bowl with the zest. Reserve (discard the zested and squeezed lime).

Combine the white chocolate chips and the cream in a small heatproof bowl and set over a small saucepan of barely simmering water. Cook, stirring frequently, until the white chocolate is melted and the mixture is very smooth. Take the pan off the heat and add the reserved lime zest and juice, stirring well to incorporate. Transfer to a squeeze bottle. Cool thoroughly before using as a drizzle. (You can set it in the refrigerator to thicken it up a little more quickly. If it thickens too much, stand the squeeze bottle in hot water for 1 to 2 minutes to soften to a squirtable consistency, then shake well before dispensing.)

Keep in the refrigerator for up to 1 week.

Bitsy Brunettes

Classic walnut brownie perfection.

1 cup all-purpose flour

½ teaspoon baking powder

⅛ teaspoon fine sea salt

4 ounces (1 stick) unsalted butter, melted

½ cup packed dark brown sugar

1 cup bittersweet chocolate chips

1 large egg

1½ teaspoons vanilla extract

½ cup chopped walnuts

Dark Chocolate Glaze, optional (page 181)

equipment

Heavyweight nonstick 24-cavity mini muffin pan

Preheat the oven to 350°F with a rack positioned in the center.

Sift the flour, baking powder, and salt together into a small bowl and set aside.

Combine the melted butter and sugar in a large bowl and whisk together until smooth and creamy.

Melt the chocolate chips in a heatproof bowl over a small saucepan of barely simmering water, stirring occasionally, until very smooth.

Add the chocolate to the butter mixture, whisking until smooth and well blended. Add the egg and vanilla, whisking to combine, then add the flour mixture and stir to incorporate. Fold in the nuts.

Scoop the dough into the prepared baking pan, dividing evenly among the 24 cups.

Bake about 8 minutes, just until the edges of the brownies begin pulling away from the pan.

Set the pan on a wire rack and let the brownies cool all the way to room temperature. Use a butter knife to gently ease each brownie out of the pan. Invert and serve flat side up, drizzled with dark chocolate glaze, if using.

Chocolate-Chili Brownie Bites

A whisper of smoky heat from chipotle chili powder gives these treats a little kick, a delicious accent to the chocolate. I like to call them *zingare*. Back in the eighties when my girlfriends and I would get dressed up to go out, our parents would see us with our teased-up crazy-curly brunette mops (talk about some big hair!), big-ass hoop earrings, bright red lipstick, and say "Look at you girls . . . like the *zingara*," meaning fiery gypsy girl—dark and lookin' like she's got a bite.

• MAKES 2 DOZEN •

1 cup flour

½ teaspoon baking powder

¼ to ½ teaspoon chipotle chili powder (use the smaller amount if you want just a whisper of heat)

⅛ teaspoon fine sea salt

4 ounces (1 stick) unsalted butter, melted

½ cup packed dark brown sugar

1½ cups bittersweet chocolate chips, divided

1 large egg

1½ teaspoons vanilla extract

equipment

Heavyweight nonstick 24-cavity mini muffin pan

Preheat the oven to 350°F with a rack positioned in the center.

Sift the flour, baking powder, chili powder, and salt together into a small bowl and set aside.

Combine the melted butter and sugar in a large bowl and whisk together until smooth and creamy.

Melt 1 cup of the chocolate chips in a heatproof bowl over a small saucepan of barely simmering water.

Add the melted chocolate to the butter mixture, whisking until smooth and well blended. Then whisk in the egg and vanilla followed by the flour mixture. Fold in the chocolate chips.

Scoop the dough into the prepared baking pan, dividing evenly among the 24 cups.

Bake about 8 minutes, just until the edges of the brownies begin pulling away from the pan. Set the pan on a wire rack and let the brownies cool all the way to room temperature, then use a butter knife to ease each brownie out of the pan.

Mother's Day

Spring is such a season of beginnings, a perfect time for recognition of motherhood. Mother's Day in May is one of the big holidays of the season in my family. I love to have the opportunity to honor my mom and my mother-in-law, who have both given us so very much. Here, on pages 120 and 122, are two very special traditional springtime recipes, handed down to me by each of them: an Italian Easter pie and a Lebanese pudding, *sneyniyeh,* that is traditionally served at important rites of passage, including when a baby cuts his or her first tooth, and for the Forty Day Mass, when the soul is passing into the afterlife (it is also known as *burbara* and is served in celebration of the feast of Saint Barbara on December 4.)

Both of the recipes use whole wheat kernels (aka wheat berries), wheat being, along with eggs and dairy, a food symbolic of birth/rebirth/renewal/new life. Pearled wheat is a particular kind of wheat berry—from soft white winter wheat that has been hulled but is otherwise whole (not "pearl wheat couscous")—seek out the Cedar brand from Phoenicia foods. Also note that the grains have to be soaked 8 hours or overnight, longer if not pearled.

Nonni Maria's Ricotta Wheat Easter Pies
Pastiera Napoletana

Rustica Pastry (page 178)

FILLING

¼ cup pearl wheat or wheat berries, rinsed, drained, and carefully picked over for tiny stones or harvest residue

1 cup whole-milk ricotta

½ cup granulated sugar

1 large egg, beaten

½ teaspoon grated orange zest

½ teaspoon vanilla extract

¼ teaspoon orange extract

2 tablespoons diced candied citron (readily available online; found at Italian specialty markets and in the baking aisle of many supermarkets at holiday time), or 2 tablespoons mini semisweet chocolate chips

1 egg white, for brushing

¼ cup coarse raw sugar for sprinkling

equipment

Electric mixer

One 12-cavity standard muffin pan

4½- to 5-inch round cutter, or a glass, can, or bowl with an opening of that diameter

Small pastry tamper, optional

One large rimmed baking sheet

To soak the pearl wheat, in a small bowl combine the grains with enough cold water to cover by 2 inches. Put the bowl in the refrigerator and let soak 8 hours or overnight in cold water, stored in the refrigerator (if the wheat berries are whole, or unpearled, soak 2 nights, changing water once).

To cook the wheat, drain and rinse the grains and combine with 1 cup fresh cold water in a small heavy bottom saucepan. Bring to a boil, then lower the heat to low and simmer until the wheat is puffed up and tender on the outside but still a little chewy in the middle, approximately 10 minutes. Drain the wheat and set it aside to cool to room temperature.

To make the filling, combine the ricotta and sugar in a large bowl and beat with an electric mixer at medium speed until smooth and creamy. Add the egg, orange zest, and extracts and beat just until uniformly incorporated. Then fold in the cooled wheat and the citron. (The filling can be made 1 day ahead and kept in an airtight container in the refrigerator.)

Use nonstick cooking spray or a vegetable oil in a misting bottle to lightly coat the baking pan.

To form the pie shells, roll out 1 disk of dough between 2 pieces of parchment paper to an even thickness of ⅛ inch. Use a 4½- to 5-inch cutter to cut 6 rounds. Gather up the dough scraps, pat together, wrap tightly, and reserve in the refrigerator (you will use it to make the lattice tops). Carefully transfer each round to the baking pans, using a pastry tamper or your fingertips to neatly mold each circle into the pan. Use scissors or a small sharp knife to cut away any excess dough. If the dough tears when you are fitting it into the pan, no worries; you can easily patch it back together. It will hold and not show. (This dough bakes up most tender if kept cool until it goes into the oven, so once you have formed all

12 shells, transfer the muffin pan to the refrigerator while you roll out and cut the strips for the lattice.)

Preheat the oven to 350°F with a rack positioned in the center.

To cut the dough for the lattice tops, roll out the reserved dough trimmings between sheets of parchment into a rectangle about 6 inches across and about 12 inches long, using the flat edge of a large knife to straighten the edges as you roll the rectangle to an even thickness of ⅛ inch. Then use the knife, or a pastry cutter or pizza wheel (and a ruler or straight edge if you like), to cut the rectangle in half lengthwise and into thirds crosswise. This will give you 6 squares of dough. Cut each rectangle lengthwise into 8 narrow strips.

Scoop ¼ cup of the ricotta filling into the chilled pastry shells (I like to use a cookie or ice cream scoop to keep things tidy).

To weave the lattice tops, lay 2 strips parallel across each tartlet, spacing evenly. Fold back every other strip halfway. Lay a third pastry strip across the middle of the tartlet, perpendicular to the first strips. Unfold the strips and fold back the alternates. Repeat with a second perpendicular strip of dough to complete the lattice. Use scissors to trim the ends of the strips flush with the edge of the bottom crust. Fold back the rim of the shell over the edge of the strips and crimp to secure.

Whisk the egg white with 1 tablespoon water. Lightly brush the pastry lattices with the egg wash, then sprinkle with the coarse sugar.

Set the pan on a baking sheet (this will make it easier to get it in and out of the oven and to rotate for even baking). Bake the pies 25 to 30 minutes, or until the pastry is light golden brown and the filling is firm but still moist, rotating the pans halfway through the baking time.

Set the baking sheet on a wire rack and let the pies cool to room temperature. Run the tip of a small sharp knife around the top outer edge of each pie to make sure the crust is not stuck to the rim of the pan. Then carefully lift the pies out of the pans. Serve at room temperature.

Teta Melake's Lebanese Wheat Berry Pudding

Sneyniyeh or Burbara

¾ cup pearl wheat or wheat berries, rinsed, drained, and carefully picked over for tiny stones or harvest residue

¾ cup blanched slivered almonds

¾ cup coarsely chopped walnuts

¾ cup pistachios

¾ cup pine nuts

½ cup granulated sugar

1½ tablespoons ground anise seed

1½ tablespoons ground fennel seed

1½ teaspoons cinnamon

½ teaspoon ground ginger

¼ teaspoon nutmeg

¾ cup raisins

Combine the wheat berries in a medium saucepan with cold water (to cover by 2 inches), bring to a boil, and then simmer for about 1 hour, stirring occasionally to prevent scorching. Remove from heat and allow to stand 5 hours or overnight. (The berries will absorb most of the water.)

In small, separate containers or bowls, pour warm water over each type of the nuts and let soak for a few hours. (This can also be done overnight; rinse and add fresh cool water if it gets murky.)

Add 2 cups water to the soaked and reserved wheat berries. Stir in the sugar, anise, fennel, cinnamon, ginger, and nutmeg. Bring the mixture to a boil, then lower the heat and simmer for 30 minutes, or until the mixture reaches a pudding-like consistency and the wheat kernels are tender but not mushy. Remove the pan from the heat and mix in ½ cup of the raisins and ½ cup of each of the nuts (drain them first).

Serve warm, cold, or at room temperature, garnished with the reserved raisins and nuts. (The pudding can be kept in an airtight container in the refrigerator for 5 days.)

Peace Offerings

There is nothing like beautiful treats lovingly made to smooth ruffled feathers. I always say we eat first with our eyes, and the visual is truly part of this gesture. Making something so lovely is healing, and receiving it is healing—from the moment it is seen, through to when it is actually eaten.

My number-one recommendation for desserts with serious peacemaking potential is anything involving orange flower water. This elixir is distilled from the petals of orange blossoms, and it has an amazing, uplifting fragrance—very subtle, very powerful. The delicate, exotic perfume transports you to another plane of existence. If this sounds mystical, well, it is! Make it your go-to for making amends anytime there's been a spat among girlfriends, some marital tension, a misunderstanding with the mother-in-law, or just a little something "off" at the office.

Desserts with orange flower water power: Doves' Nests (page 108)—Bird of peace symbolism, plus soothingly sweet-tart apricot flavor. Also: the three other birds' nests recipes (pages 106-110), and Baklawa (page 37)—so sumptuous!

Then there's chocolate. Chocolate Custard Tartlets (page 94) could really brighten a bad day. And there is nothing like my Chocolate Tiramisu (page 153) to provide a great little pick-me-up—given that's what "tira-mi-su" actually means. It's the perfectly elegant combination of silky zabaglione and decadent chocolate with just a hint of espresso. Sure to chase anyone's blues away.

Any one of these confections will make the receiver feel like they mean the world to you because of how much love and care you put into making them.

{ summer }

In the summer Jersey comes alive in an amazing way. Growing up, my parents never really liked using the air conditioner; they said it was bad for their bones. Okay, what do I know? But it didn't matter anyway because we all spent so much time outdoors. And getting that evening summer breeze was always a treat. Because along with the breeze came the intoxicating sounds of summer. When the weather warmed up everybody opened up their windows and just like that we were no longer sealed off from one another indoors. Life spilled out through all the windows and screen doors, and all the activity going on outside came in, too—kids running through the backyards until long after dark, families having meals out on their patios, cars zipping by with radios playing and teenagers hooting and hollering—I remember lying in bed listening to it all when I was little.

Before long I was one of those teens, and in true Jersey Italian style, right on through my early twenties, summer was all about where the party was "down the shore" (up in north Jersey that's what we call it; in south Jersey they just say "at the beach"). And even since I've been settled with my own family, summer is still pretty manic, but in the best possible way—it's a crazy, exciting, get-it-while-you-can energy. There are only so many weekends to do the barbecues and the weekends down the shore and the pool parties and everything. After a while the weekdays just become one big weekend. And why not? We get three good months; enjoy every minute is our motto. Is there a big heat wave coming? How jammed will the Garden State Parkway be on Friday night and again on Sunday? Are there thunderstorms in the forecast?

It's hectic, but it sure is fun. And I love to dish up delicious cooling treats, sit back, and savor the sweetness.

Tony's
Lemon Ice

page {131}

Granita Splendida

I n the summertime when Rosie and I were kids, my dad would often sit back in his chair after dinner, pucker up his mouth, make this little lip-smacking sound, and say, "Y'know what? Let's go get an ice." Off we'd go, Daddy, Ma, Rosie, and me (my brothers were quite a bit older and always off doing their own thing by then), to one of the stands up the street. Nothing delivers a moment of sweet escape from summer heat and humidity like an ice, and lemon was my father's absolute favorite. The thing was, he was the serious type, a big, strong and very authoritative figure, so it was really something for me to see him slurping the slushy lemon ice out of the little paper cup. It made him so happy, almost like a little kid, and for me to see that when I was a little kid myself made me realize that he had once been a child, just like me. Knocking back our ices together it even felt for a few moments like we were both kids, together, equals in the joy of a simple summer treat.

Granita *a Modo Mio* (My Way)

I always use an ice-cream maker to make granita, but you certainly don't have to. The traditional method is to put the liquid mixture in a shallow pan in the freezer, scrape it with a fork or a big metal spoon to break up the ice after 1 hour, and do that again every 30 minutes or so for another 2 to 3 hours to achieve a nice flaky consistency. Rather than figure out a way to free up that much space in my freezer and do all those rounds of scraping, I prefer to make the syrup ahead of time, then throw it into the ice-cream maker about 30 minutes before I want to serve, so it is slushy and spoonable, in little glasses or footed 2- to 3-ounce dessert bowls.

Tony's Lemon Ice

Named for my dad, Anthony Pierri, Jersey's biggest-ever fan of the lemon ice, this is a delectably sweet-tart, super-cooling summer treat. I love to serve it in hollowed-out lemon halves. It is also lovely in little shot glasses with teeny espresso spoons. But little paper cups are great, too, for that old-school Italian ice-stand vibe. Pointy-bottomed paper snow-cone cups are also a fun way to go.

• MAKES ABOUT 1 QUART •

6 to 8 large lemons, for zest of 4 lemons and 1½ cups freshly squeezed juice

3 cups water

1¼ cups granulated sugar

equipment

Ice-cream maker (at least 1½-quart capacity recommended)

Microplane

Zest 2 of the lemons with a vegetable peeler for long strips of lemon peel (for easy skimming later). Reserve.

Use a microplane to finely grate the zest of 2 more lemons; reserve (keep in a small airtight container in the refrigerator if saving for more than 1 hour).

Juice the zested lemons and additional lemons as needed for a total of 1½ cups juice. Cover and chill for 1 hour or up to 3 days.

In a medium, heavy-bottom saucepan, heat the water and sugar, stirring until sugar is dissolved, about 5 minutes. Transfer the syrup to a bowl and stir in the reserved long strips of lemon peel, then cover and chill 6 hours or up to 3 days.

Skim and discard lemon peel from syrup. Stir in the reserved grated lemon zest and lemon juice.

Pour the mixture into the freezer bowl of an ice-cream maker. Run the machine until the granita is frozen and slushy and spoonable, 20 to 25 minutes. Serve immediately.

Espresso with a Shot (or Not)

A fantastic cool-me-down and pick-me-up in one, this slushy but sophisticated treat infuses sweet, strong coffee flavor with the subtle licorice perfume of star anise. Not that it needs anything else, but in Rome they often serve espresso granita *con panna*—layered with whipped heavy cream. I'm just sayin' . . .

1 cup water

½ cup granulated sugar

6 star anise

2½ cups freshly brewed best-quality espresso

equipment

Ice-cream maker (at least 1½-quart capacity recommended)

To make the anise syrup, combine the water, sugar, and star anise in a medium heavy-bottom saucepan. Bring to a boil over medium heat then reduce the heat to low and simmer for about 5 minutes, or until reduced by half.

Pour through a strainer into a large heatproof bowl (discard the star anise pods). Add the espresso and mix well. Cover and chill for 6 hours or up to 3 days.

Make the granita about 30 minutes before you want to serve it. Pour the chilled espresso mixture into the freezer bowl of an ice-cream maker and churn until the granita is frozen and slushy and spoonable, 20 to 30 minutes.

Pink Lady

Fresh mint and mint extract bring out the sweet, tart flavor of ruby grapefruit in a wonderful way that makes this granita a surprising and incredibly refreshing finish to any summer meal. Plus the rosy color is just gorgeous.

1½ cups water

1 cup granulated sugar

¼ cup rinsed fresh mint leaves, plus sprigs for garnish

2 cups freshly squeezed pink grapefruit juice, preferably ruby red (from 5 to 8 medium grapefruits)

3 teaspoons finely grated grapefruit zest

1 teaspoon pure orange extract

1 teaspoon pure mint extract

equipment

Ice-cream maker (at least 1½-quart capacity recommended)

To make the mint-infused syrup, combine the water, sugar, and mint in a medium heavy-bottom saucepan. Bring to a boil over medium heat, then reduce the heat to low and simmer until it is reduced to 1 cup, about 15 minutes.

Pour through a strainer into a large heatproof bowl. Discard mint leaves. Add grapefruit juice and zest and mix well. Stir in orange and mint extracts. Cover and chill for 6 hours or up to 3 days.

Make the granita about 30 minutes before you want to serve it. Pour the chilled juice mixture into the freezer bowl of an ice-cream maker and churn until the granita is frozen and slushy and spoonable, 20 to 30 minutes.

Bottla Red

Slushie meets sangria, cocktail meets dessert. So cooling! So delicious!

1½ cups water

1 ripe peach, sliced

1 ripe plum, sliced

¾ cup granulated sugar

1 cup your favorite red wine

1 cup orange juice or fruit juice

equipment

Ice-cream maker (at least 1½-quart capacity recommended)

In a medium, heavy-bottom saucepan, heat the water, sliced fruit, and sugar, stirring until sugar is dissolved, 5 to 10 minutes. Transfer the syrup to a bowl, then cover and chill for 6 hours or up to 3 days.

Skim and discard fruit from syrup (you should have 1 cup or so of syrup). Stir in chilled fruit juice and chilled red wine. Pour the mixture into the freezer bowl of an ice-cream maker. Run the machine until the granita is frozen and slushy and spoonable, 20 to 25 minutes. Serve immediately.

> note: If fresh fruit isn't available, you can substitute frozen: 1 cup frozen mixed berries and 1 cup frozen mango is a delicious combo.

We All Scream for Gelato!

In the summer of 1984, the ice-cream joint down the block from our house changed hands and reopened as an ice-cream shop/gelateria. (The place, Gelotti, is still there—and they were kind enough to welcome me in to make some summer desserts and serve them up to the cast, invited guests, and the public on an episode of the show in 2012.) Rosie got her first-ever job there that summer, scooping gelato. Every night the place would be hopping, the parking lot jammed with cars with the stereos cranked up and people hanging out. When Rosie had nights off, she and I would walk over for a gelato or an ice. We'd time it carefully for the peak of the evening rush, right after dinner when the place was really mobbed. See, the lines would be long so we'd get to hang out while we waited without breaking the rules (intentional hanging out being something we Pierri girls were still, at eighteen and sixteen years old, not allowed to do—we had traditional Italian parents for sure). So Ro and I would get our gelato, then, just as the sun got to sinking really low, we'd walk home. Slowly, but not too slowly—we had to be in before the streetlights came on. Unless of course we were coming home from work!

Strawberries-and-Cream

I like my *gelato alla fragola* a little on the rustic side, with bits of fresh strawberry throughout. Make sure you do the macerating step only 1 hour ahead, to extract some of the juice from the berries without softening the fruit too much. If you prefer a smooth strawberry gelato, by all means, feel free to just use all 3 cups of the strawberries in the purée at the beginning of the recipe.

• MAKES ABOUT 1 QUART •

1 quart fresh strawberries, stemmed and hulled (about 3 cups), divided

¾ cup granulated sugar, divided

¼ cup nonfat powdered milk

½ cup whole milk

½ cup heavy cream

1¼ cups half-and-half, divided

3 large egg yolks

1 tablespoon freshly squeezed lemon juice

equipment

Food processor

Electric mixer

Ice-cream maker (at least 1½-quart capacity recommended)

Use a food processor to purée 2½ cups of the strawberries. Transfer the strawberry purée to a large heavy-bottom saucepan. Add 2 tablespoons of the sugar, mix well, and bring to a simmer over medium heat. Cook about 20 minutes to reduce by half to about 1¼ cups. Remove the saucepan from the heat, let the strawberry purée cool, then transfer it to a bowl. Cover and chill thoroughly, about 1 hour.

In a separate bowl, whisk together the powdered milk, whole milk, heavy cream, and ½ cup of the half-and-half, mixing until smooth. Set aside.

Return the saucepan to the heat, pour in the remaining ¾ cup of the half-and-half, and stir in the remaining ½ cup sugar. Bring the mixture to a simmer over medium heat and cook, stirring, until the sugar is completely dissolved, about 2 minutes. Keep warm over very low heat.

In a medium bowl, beat the egg yolks with an electric mixer on low speed until uniformly thick and yellow, about 2 minutes.

To temper the egg yolks, measure out ¼ cup of the warm half-and-half mixture and, with the mixer running on low speed, gradually pour it into the egg yolks in a thin stream (this will help prevent the eggs from curdling when mixed with the larger amount of warm half-and-half).

Stir the tempered egg yolks into the half-and-half mixture in the saucepan and increase heat to medium. Cook, stirring constantly with a wooden spoon, until the mixture is thickened to a custard (at which point it will coat the back of a wooden spoon), about 5 minutes.

Remove the saucepan from the heat and whisk in the reserved powdered milk mixture. Add the chilled strawberry purée and stir until well blended. Cover and refrigerate for at least 6 hours or overnight before using the ice-cream maker.

One hour prior to using the ice-cream maker, coarsely chop the remaining ½ cup strawberries and place them in a bowl. Sprinkle with the remaining 2 tablespoons of sugar and the lemon juice, then toss well to combine. Cover and chill.

Strain the chopped, macerated strawberries over a bowl. Whisk the macerating liquid into the custard. Reserve the chopped strawberries in the refrigerator, keeping them cold until you are ready to add them to the gelato.

Turn on the ice-cream maker, pour the chilled custard into the freezer bowl, and let it mix until the custard starts to thicken, 15 to 20 minutes. Add the reserved chilled strawberries and continue mixing until the gelato has a soft, creamy texture, approximately 10 more minutes. Cover and freeze until set, about 2 hours.

> tip: For beautiful ice-cream sandwiches, layer an inch or so of strawberries-and-cream gelato between pizzelle (page 169) and freeze until firm.

Orange Dreamsicle

One of the inspirations here is an old popsicle favorite. But another is frozen custard, Jersey's own special style of soft-serve. The Kohr's stand at Franklin Avenue and the boardwalk in Seaside Heights has been a fixture since 1943. No stroll down the Seaside boardwalk would be complete without a tasty stop there, and it wouldn't be summertime DTS (down the shore) without it. Recently, like so many others in Jersey (and beyond) Kohr's has had more than their fair share of misfortune: not long after they rebuilt from Superstorm Sandy, there was a huge fire that ravaged the boardwalk all over again. But I have faith they'll be back. Jersey Strong!

• MAKES ABOUT 1 QUART •

2 cups freshly squeezed orange juice, with pulp

6 tablespoons plus ½ cup granulated sugar, divided

1¼ cups half-and-half, divided

3 large egg yolks

¼ cup nonfat powdered milk

1 cup heavy cream

½ cup whole milk

2 tablespoons vanilla extract

1 teaspoon orange extract

1 teaspoon freshly grated orange zest

equipment

Electric mixer

Ice-cream maker (at least 1½-quart capacity recommended)

Combine the juice and 6 tablespoons of the sugar in a large heavy-bottom saucepan over low heat. Bring to a simmer and cook, stirring occasionally, until the sugar is dissolved and the liquid is reduced by about half, 15 to 20 minutes (you should have 1 cup). Transfer the orange reduction to a heatproof bowl, let cool to room temperature, then cover with plastic wrap and reserve in the refrigerator. (This can be made ahead and kept in a jar in the refrigerator for several days.)

In a separate bowl, whisk together the powdered milk, heavy cream, whole milk, and ½ cup of the half-and-half, mixing until smooth. Set aside.

Return the saucepan to the heat, pour in the remaining ¾ cup half-and-half, and stir in the remaining ½ cup sugar. Bring the mixture to a simmer over medium heat and cook, stirring, until the sugar is completely dissolved, about 2 minutes. Keep warm over low heat.

In a medium bowl, beat the egg yolks with an electric mixer on low speed until uniformly thick and yellow, about 2 minutes.

Measure out ¼ cup of the warm half-and-half mixture.

With the mixer still running on low speed, gradually add the ¼ cup warm half-and-half in a thin stream (this process is called tempering and will help prevent the eggs from curdling).

Stir the tempered egg yolks into the half-and-half mixture in the saucepan and increase the heat to medium. Cook, stirring constantly with a wooden spoon until the mixture is thickened to a custard (at which point it will coat the back of wooden spoon), about 5 minutes.

Remove the pan from the heat and pour the powdered milk mixture into the custard, whisking to incorporate. Add the reserved orange reduction and the vanilla extract and orange zest and stir until well blended. Transfer the mixture to a bowl, cover tightly with plastic, and chill in the refrigerator for at least 6 hours before using the ice-cream maker. (The gelato can be prepared up to 2 days ahead.)

Turn on the ice-cream maker, pour the chilled custard into the freezer bowl, and let it mix until the custard starts to thicken, 20 to 25 minutes. Continue mixing until the gelato has a soft creamy texture, approximately 10 more minutes. Cover and freeze until set, about 2 hours.

This summer Rich and I, along with the kids, enjoyed eating our weight in gelato all over Italy.

Chocolate-Covered Cherry

Last summer in Rome I was introduced to a cherry dessert wine, Vino e Visciole, made from wild visciole cherries, when the owner of the restaurant where we were eating proudly presented us with his secret stash of the wine, along with some homemade chocolate truffles. That vino was more luscious than any chocolate-covered cherry candy I've ever had and I could not get it out of my mind! We came home to Jersey in the middle of a blistering heat wave and I came up with this recipe, so I can recreate the experience over and over and for everyone to enjoy. *Centi Anni!*

•MAKES 1 QUART•

CHOCOLATE-CHERRY SWIRL
One 4-ounce bar semisweet chocolate, chopped

¼ cup heavy cream

2 tablespoons cherry liqueur (such as Heering) or Chambord

1 tablespoon unsalted butter

1 pound dark sweet fresh cherries, pitted and coarsely chopped (4 cups)

½ cup plus 2 tablespoons granulated sugar, divided

2 tablespoons cherry liqueur (such as Heering) or Chambord

1 tablespoon freshly squeezed lemon

1¼ cups half-and-half, divided

3 large egg yolks

¼ cup nonfat powdered milk

½ cup heavy cream

½ cup whole milk

1 teaspoon vanilla extract

To make the chocolate-cherry swirl, combine the chocolate and the heavy cream in a medium heatproof bowl over a saucepan of simmering water, stirring until the chocolate is melted and the mixture is smooth. Remove from the heat and mix in the liqueur and butter, stirring until the butter is melted and incorporated. Cover and set aside to cool to room temperature. (The chocolate can be made ahead and kept in an airtight container in the refrigerator for several days. Stir to loosen before adding to the gelato.)

Combine the cherries, 2 tablespoons of the sugar, the liqueur, and the lemon juice in a large heavy-bottom saucepan and set over low heat. Bring to a simmer and cook, stirring occasionally, until the sugar is dissolved and the cherries begin to release their juice to coat the bottom of the pan, 2 to 3 minutes.

Set a wire sieve or colander over a large bowl and drain the cherries. Reserve the juices. Transfer the drained fruit to another bowl, cover with plastic wrap, and chill in the refrigerator.

Return the cherry juices to the saucepan and heat to a low simmer. Cook for about 5 minutes or until reduced by half (you want to end up with ¼ cup juice). Pour the reduction into a heatproof bowl and set aside.

In a mixing bowl, whisk together the powdered milk, heavy cream, whole milk, and ½ cup of the half-and-half, mixing until smooth. Set aside.

Return the saucepan to the heat (be sure to let it cool a bit), pour in the remaining ¾ cup of the half-and-half, and stir in the remaining ½ cup sugar. Bring the mixture to a simmer over medium heat and cook, stirring, until the sugar is completely dissolved, about 2 minutes. Keep warm over low heat.

In a medium bowl, beat the egg yolks with an electric mixer on low speed until uniformly thick and yellow, about 2 minutes.

Measure out ¼ cup of the warm half-and-half mixture.

With the electric mixer still running on low speed, gradually add the ¼ cup warm half-and-half in a thin stream (this process is called tempering and will help prevent the eggs from curdling).

Stir the tempered egg yolks into the half-and-half mixture in the saucepan and increase the heat to medium. Cook, stirring constantly with a wooden spoon, until the mixture is thickened to a custard (at which point it will coat the back of a wooden spoon), about 5 minutes.

Remove the pan from the heat and pour the powdered milk mixture into the custard, whisking to incorporate. Add the reserved cherry syrup and vanilla extract and stir until well blended. Cover and refrigerate for at least 6 hours before using the ice-cream maker.

Turn on the ice-cream maker, pour the chilled custard into the freezer bowl, and let it mix for about 15 minutes, until the custard starts to thicken. Add the reserved cherries and continue mixing until the gelato has a soft, creamy texture, approximately 10 more minutes.

To add the chocolate-cherry swirl, working quickly, scoop ⅓ of the gelato out of the ice-cream maker and transfer into an airtight plastic container. Use a teaspoon to drop ¼ of the chocolate mixture into the gelato in different places, then use a knife to swirl the chocolate, connecting the patches of chocolate but not mixing them into the gelato. Repeat the process twice to add and swirl the remaining gelato. Reserve the last quarter of the chocolate to drizzle onto the finished gelato. Cover the gelato with an airtight lid and freeze until the gelato sets a bit, approximately 2 hours.

Serve with the reserved chocolate-cherry swirl.

Tanned and Salty

Sure, I could just call this "Chocolate Gelato with Sea-Salted Caramel Swirl," but that wouldn't get across the inspiration behind the recipe: Belmar, New Jersey, back in the day, when it was all about getting our young bods on the beach. Sun-kissed, sea-sprayed, sexy summer fun. Delicious.

note: You will need a large container—deep and wide enough to give you room to swirl the caramel into the gelato—with an airtight lid.

•MAKES ABOUT 1½ QUARTS•

1 cup bittersweet chocolate chips

½ cup heavy cream

¼ cup nonfat powdered milk

½ cup whole milk

1¼ cups half-and-half, divided

½ cup granulated sugar

3 large egg yolks

1 teaspoon vanilla extract

Caramel Swirl (recipe follows)

1 to 2 teaspoons fleur de sel or other flaky sea salt

equipment

Electric mixer

Ice-cream maker (at least 1½-quart capacity recommended)

Chop the chocolate into small pieces and transfer to a large heat-proof mixing bowl. Heat the heavy cream to a simmer and pour over the chocolate. Let sit 5 minutes, then stir until silky smooth, 1 to 2 minutes. Set aside.

In a separate bowl, whisk together the powdered milk, whole milk, and ½ cup of the half-and-half, mixing until smooth. Set aside.

Combine the sugar and the remaining ¾ cup half-and-half in a large, heavy-bottom saucepan. Bring the mixture to a simmer over medium heat and cook, stirring often, until the sugar is completely dissolved, about 2 minutes. Keep warm over very low heat.

In a medium bowl, beat the egg yolks with an electric mixer on low speed until uniformly thick and yellow, about 2 minutes.

To temper the egg yolks, measure out ¼ cup of the warm sugar and half-and-half mixture and, with the mixer running on low speed, gradually pour it into the egg yolks in a thin stream (this will help prevent the eggs from curdling when mixed with the larger amount of warm half-and-half).

Stir the tempered egg yolks into the sugar and half-and-half mixture in the saucepan and increase heat to medium. Cook, stirring constantly with a wooden spoon, until the mixture is thickened to a custard (at which point it will coat the back of a wooden spoon), about 5 minutes.

Remove the pan from the heat and whisk in the powdered milk mixture. Add the custard mixture to the reserved chocolate mixture, using a flexible rubber spatula to mix well and scrape down the sides of the bowl to make sure all of the chocolate is fully incorporated. Stir in the vanilla, cover tightly with plastic, and chill in the refrigerator for at least 6 hours or overnight before using the ice-cream maker.

Prepare the caramel sauce and set aside to cool to room temperature.

Turn on the ice-cream maker and pour the chilled custard into the freezer bowl and let mix approximately 20 minutes, or just until the gelato has a soft, creamy texture. This is the time to add in the caramel swirl.

Sprinkle the caramel with sea salt to taste, stirring to incorporate and loosen the sauce so that it will be easy to drop into the gelato.

Working quickly, scoop ⅓ of the gelato into a large wide plastic container with an airtight lid and use a large spoon to drop ⅓ of the caramel in different places, then use a knife to swirl the caramel, connecting the patches of caramel but not mixing them into the gelato. Repeat with remaining gelato and caramel. Cover with lid and freeze until set, approximately 2 hours.

Caramel Swirl

1 cup granulated sugar

¼ cup water

½ cup heavy cream, at room temperature

2 teaspoons vanilla extract

Combine the sugar and water in a small saucepan and bring to a boil over medium-high heat. Cook, without stirring, until the mixture begins to turn brown, about 5 minutes, then stir gently with a wooden spoon to distribute the color evenly. Keeping a close watch on the saucepan and giving the syrup an occasional stir, continue cooking a few more minutes until the mixture is a deep, rich brown. Carefully pour in the heavy cream in a thin stream. The mixture will bubble up, but will then subside if you keep stirring in the trickle of cream. Take the saucepan off the heat and add the vanilla. Let cool to room temperature before using.

Chocolate
Tiramisu
page {153}

"Pick-Me-Up" (Italiano)

On a family trip to Italy when I was eleven and my little sister, Rosie, was about nine, the two of us stayed overnight with Zia Anna, my father's older sister, on her farm in the countryside of Campania while my parents traveled around visiting other relatives. When we got up in the morning, Zia Anna wanted to serve us breakfast. The traditional morning meal would have been just biscotti dipped in warm milk, but Zia Anna wanted to do something special and "American" for us. When she asked if we'd like some eggs, we said, "Sure." Well, I thought she meant scrambled or sunny-side up. Next thing I know, Zia Anna fetches a few eggs from the chicken coop, cracks them into a glass, whips them into a froth with some marsala and a little sugar, and sets the glass in front of me. Not knowing what else to do and terrified of being rude, I pick up the glass, drinking down the raw eggs and praying that they won't come right back up. Rosie, being Rosie, takes one look and says, "I ain't drinkin' that." And my aunt says, in Italian, "Oh, would you like me to cook it?" And Rosie gets hers cooked! That right there is a typical Kathy-and-Rosie story, my friends.

It wasn't until many years later that I realized that this was my first encounter with zabaglione: the combination of eggs, marsala, and sugar that is so central to the layered wonderfulness of tiramisu. (I still prefer mine cooked!)

My father adored his eldest sister, Anna, and so did I. I took this picture of her as I was leaving the last time I visited her, not long before she passed.

Tiramisu Tradizionale

Classic Tiramisu

Tiramisu is one of those classic desserts that is really fun to serve because people love it but are accustomed to less-than-stellar versions, so when they get a taste of the real thing it pretty much blows their minds. It is not at all difficult to make fantastic tiramisu, but it does take a little time and care. A couple of key pointers for traditional tiramisu: great coffee flavor is essential, so be sure to go for top-quality in both your coffee (ideally espresso) and your coffee liqueur (I prefer Tia Maria and Trader Vic's Kona). For this and my other tiramisu variations, assemble at least one full day ahead, so it sets up nicely and the flavors meld. Note that the number of ladyfinger cookies needed, and how to cut them up, depends upon the size and dimensions of your serving vessels. Lastly, serve in glass dishes to show off the beautiful layers!

MAKES 12 TO 18

¼ cup coffee liqueur, such as Trader Vic's Kona or Tia Maria

3 large egg yolks, at room temperature

¼ cup granulated sugar

1 cup freshly brewed espresso

¼ cup dry marsala wine

½ cup cold heavy cream

One 8-ounce tub mascarpone cheese, at room temperature

36 crisp Italian ladyfingers (*savoiardi*), plus more as needed

Chantilly Cream (page 183), for serving

Cocoa powder or grated chocolate, for serving

To make the zabaglione, combine the egg yolks, marsala, and sugar in a heatproof bowl. Set the bowl over a saucepan of barely simmering water (make sure the bowl is not touching the water) and beat constantly with a handheld electric mixer (or a whisk) for 6 to 8 minutes. As it cooks, the mixture will become frothy and thicken, initially turning almost spongy, then taking on a smoother consistency and becoming thick enough to form a ribbon (rather than dripping) from the beaters to the surface of the custard. Remove the pan from the heat and set aside to cool. (Can be made up to 2 days ahead and kept in an airtight container in the refrigerator.)

To make the soaking liquid, combine the espresso and the liqueur in a shallow bowl. Stir to combine and set aside. (The soaking liquid can be made ahead and kept in an airtight container in the refrigerator for several days.)

When you are ready to assemble the tiramisu, drain any watery liquid from the top of the mascarpone, give it a stir to soften, and stir the mascarpone into the zabaglione until just combined.

(Recipe continued on next page)

equipment

Handheld electric mixer

Twelve to eighteen 3- to 4-ounce
glass serving dishes

Pastry bag and large round tip,
optional

In a separate large bowl, whip the cream to stiff peaks, then gradually add the mascarpone-zabaglione mixture to the whipped cream a little at a time, folding gently to combine.

Cut the ladyfingers into pieces as needed to fit the serving dishes you are using (you may need short little pieces for the bottom and middle layers, but longer pieces to stand up around the sides of the dishes). Dip the cookies in the espresso soaking liquid, letting them absorb some of the syrup but not so much that they go soggy—al dente toward the center is good.

Lay a soaked ladyfinger flat in the bottom of each dish, then stand a few cookie pieces on end (cut sides down) around the outside of the dish (leave space between them; you want the velvety cream to peek through). Use a pastry bag to pipe in a layer of the mascarpone-zabaglione-cream mixture (you can spoon it in instead, but piping is much neater and easier). Top with another piece of soaked ladyfinger, then another layer of mascarpone cream. Repeat as needed, depending on the size and shape of your serving dishes.

Refrigerate, covered, for at least 5 hours or overnight. (Tiramisu can be made ahead and kept in the refrigerator for up to 3 days. These also freeze beautifully; thaw overnight in the refrigerator.)

Let sit at room temperature for 30 minutes before serving, topped with Chantilly cream and sprinkled with cocoa and/or grated chocolate.

Cioccolato
Chocolate Tiramisu

For my chocolate version of tiramisu, I use chocolate liqueur in place of both the marsala in the zabaglione and the Tia Maria in the soak for the ladyfingers. I also add layers of rich, velvety ganache. Dreamy!

•MAKES 12 TO 18•

3 large egg yolks, at room temperature

¼ cup plus 1 tablespoon granulated sugar, divided

¼ cup plus 2 tablespoons chocolate liqueur, preferably Godiva Dark Chocolate, divided

1 cup brewed espresso coffee

One 6-ounce bar bittersweet (60% cacao) chocolate

1 cup cold heavy cream, divided

4 tablespoons (½ stick) unsalted butter

One 8-ounce tub mascarpone cheese, at room temperature

½ teaspoon vanilla extract

36 crisp Italian ladyfingers (*savoiardi*), plus more if needed

Chantilly Cream (page 183), for serving

Cocoa powder and/or grated dark or milk chocolate, for serving

equipment

Handheld electric mixer

Pastry bag and large round tip

Twelve to eighteen small 3- to 4-ounce glass serving dishes

To make the zabaglione, combine the egg yolks, ¼ cup of the sugar, and ¼ cup of the liqueur in a heatproof bowl. Set the bowl over a saucepan of barely simmering water (make sure the bowl is not touching the water) and beat constantly with a handheld electric mixer (or a whisk) for 8 to 10 minutes. As it cooks, the mixture will become frothy and thicken, initially turning almost spongy, then taking on a smoother consistency and becoming thick enough to form a ribbon (rather than dripping) from the beaters to the surface of the custard. Remove the pan from the heat and set aside to cool to room temperature. (The zabaglione can be made up to 2 days ahead and kept in an airtight container in the refrigerator.)

To make the soaking liquid, stir together the hot espresso and the chocolate liqueur in a shallow bowl; let cool to room temperature. (This can be made ahead and kept in a jar in the refrigerator for several days.)

To make the ganache, finely chop the chocolate and put it in a medium heatproof bowl. Combine ½ cup of the heavy cream with the butter in a small saucepan and heat over medium heat, stirring constantly. Pour the hot cream mixture over the chocolate. Add the remaining 2 tablespoons of liqueur and stir just to incorporate. Let sit 5 minutes, then stir until smooth. Cool to room temperature. (The ganache can be made ahead and kept in an airtight container in the refrigerator for a week. Bring to room temperature before layering into the tiramisu.)

When you are ready to assemble the tiramisu, drain any watery liquid from the top of the mascarpone, give it a stir to soften, then stir it into the zabaglione until just combined. Whip the remaining

½ cup cream to stiff peaks in a large bowl, then gradually add the mascarpone-zabaglione mixture to the whipped cream a little at a time, folding gently to combine.

Cut the ladyfingers into pieces as needed to fit the serving dishes you are using (you may need short little pieces for the bottom and middle layers, but longer pieces to stand up around the sides of the dishes). Dip the cookies in the espresso soaking liquid, letting them absorb some of the syrup but not so much that they go soggy—al dente toward the center is good.

Lay a soaked ladyfinger flat in the bottom of each serving dish, then stand a few cookie pieces on end (cut sides down) around the outside of the dish (leave space between them; you want the velvety cream to peek through). Use a pastry bag to pipe in a layer of the mascarpone mixture (you can spoon it in instead, but piping is much neater and easier). Use another pastry bag (or a heavyweight zip-top bag with one of the bottom corners cut off) to pipe in a thin layer of ganache. Follow that with another ladyfinger and repeat layering to fill the dishes. (This can be made ahead and kept in the refrigerator for up to 3 days. These also freeze beautifully; thaw overnight in the refrigerator.)

Let sit at room temperature for 30 minutes before serving. Top with Chantilly cream, a dusting of cocoa, and a sprinkling of grated chocolate.

> tip: Tiramisu, especially the more complex variations, breaks down into components that are easy to prepare one at a time and keep well for days, so I typically make it in stages and hold off on assembly until the day before I'm going to serve it.

Capri Mia
Limoncello Tiramisu

I love everything lemon, and first discovered limoncello—the most summery liqueur imaginable—on a trip to the island of Capri on Italy's Amalfi Coast many years ago. Lemon curd is one of my specialties, so creating a version with limoncello was one of the first ways I came up with for using the liqueur in desserts. One thing led to another, as it goes with me in the kitchen, and before long the limoncello curd became a limoncello tiramisu. I am just going to come right out and say it: this one is a real showstopper. Ethereal, lemony perfection.

—•MAKES 12 TO 18•—

5 large egg yolks, at room temperature, divided

½ cup plus 2 tablespoons granulated sugar, divided

1½ teaspoons finely grated lemon zest, divided

¾ cup plus 2 tablespoons freshly squeezed lemon juice, divided

2 tablespoons butter, diced

¾ cup limoncello liqueur, divided

One 8-ounce tub mascarpone cheese, at room temperature

½ cup cold heavy cream

36 crisp Italian ladyfingers (*savoiardi*), plus more as needed

Chantilly Cream (page 183), for serving

Lemon zest, preferably in long thin strips, for serving

Mint sprigs, for serving

Chopped toasted pistachios, for serving

To make the limoncello curd, in a medium heatproof bowl whisk 2 of the egg yolks together with ¼ cup of the sugar, ½ teaspoon of the lemon zest, and 2 tablespoons of the lemon juice until blended. Set the bowl over a saucepan of barely simmering water and continue whisking until the mixture has thickened to a custard consistency (coating a wooden spoon), 7 to 10 minutes.

Remove the mixture from the heat and stir in the butter a few little pieces at a time, making sure each addition is fully incorporated before adding the next. Stir in 2 tablespoons of the limoncello and set the curd aside to cool completely, then chill thoroughly. (Can be made ahead and kept in an airtight container in the refrigerator for several days; stir until smooth before using).

To make the limoncello soaking liquid, in a saucepan combine the remaining ¾ cup lemon juice with ½ cup of the limoncello, ¼ cup of the sugar, and ½ cup water. Bring to a boil, stirring to dissolve the sugar. Cook for 5 minutes (this allows alcohol to evaporate), then take the pan off the stove and let the soaking liquid cool to room temperature. (Can be made a day ahead and kept in a jar in the refrigerator.)

To make the limoncello zabaglione, in a heatproof bowl whisk together the remaining 3 egg yolks, 2 tablespoons sugar, and ¼ cup limoncello until well blended. Set the bowl over barely simmering water and beat constantly with a handheld electric mixer (or a whisk) for 8 to 10 minutes. As it cooks, the mixture will become frothy and thicken, initially turning almost spongy, then taking on a smoother consistency and becoming thick enough to form a ribbon (rather than dripping) from the beaters to the surface of the custard. Remove the pan from the heat and set aside to cool. (Can be made up to 2 days ahead and kept in an airtight container in the refrigerator.)

When you are ready to assemble the tiramisu, drain any watery liquid from the top of the mascarpone. Put the mascarpone in a large mixing bowl and give it a good stir to soften. Add the remaining teaspoon of lemon zest to the bowl and stir until creamy, then use a flexible rubber spatula to fold in the lemon curd until just combined. Add the zabaglione in thirds, folding gently with a large rubber spatula between each addition.

In a separate large bowl, whip the heavy cream to stiff peaks, then gradually add the mascarpone-zabaglione mixture to the whipped cream a little at a time, folding gently to combine.

Cut the ladyfingers into pieces as needed to fit the serving dishes you are using. Dip the cookies in the soaking liquid, letting them absorb some of the syrup but not so much that they go soggy—al dente toward the center is good.

Lay a soaked ladyfinger flat in the bottom of each serving dish, then stand a few cookie pieces on end around the outside of the dish (leave space between them; you want the velvety cream to peek through). Use a pastry bag to pipe in a layer of the mascarpone-zabaglione-cream mixture (you can spoon it in instead, but piping is much neater and easier). Top with another piece of soaked ladyfinger, then another layer of mascarpone cream. Repeat as needed, depending on the size and shape of your serving dishes.

Refrigerate, covered, for at least 6 hours or overnight. (This can be made ahead and kept in the refrigerator for up to 3 days. This dessert also freezes beautifully; thaw overnight in the refrigerator.)

Let sit at room temperature for 30 minutes before serving, topped with Chantilly cream and sprinkled with lemon zest, chopped pistachios, and mint sprigs.

Fuzzy Navel

Peach Tiramisu

Last summer I had a big bowl of luscious Jersey peaches in the kitchen that were perfectly ripe—more than we could possibly eat before they were past their prime. I got to thinking of fuzzy navels—the silly peach schnapps cocktail my girlfriends and I all loved as wild young things down the shore, back in the eighties. I remembered a version I once had in a bar in Atlantic City that had lemonade in addition to the schnapps and orange juice. So I whipped up a batch of that limoncello curd from my limoncello tiramisu recipe and experimented away. . . .

•MAKES 12 TO 18•

5 large egg yolks, divided

½ teaspoon lemon zest

2 tablespoons lemon juice

½ cup plus 2 tablespoons granulated sugar, divided

2 tablespoons butter, diced

6 tablespoons peach schnapps, divided

1½ cups freshly squeezed orange juice

½ cup Cointreau or other orange-flavored liqueur

½ vanilla bean

2 teaspoons peach extract, divided

½ cup cold heavy cream

36 crisp Italian ladyfinger cookies (*savoiardi*), plus more as needed

4 to 6 ripe fresh peaches

½ lemon

One 8-ounce tub mascarpone cheese, at room temperature

1½ teaspoons orange zest

To make the curd, in a medium heatproof bowl, whisk 2 of the egg yolks together with the lemon zest, lemon juice, and ¼ cup of the sugar until blended. Set the bowl over a saucepan of barely simmering water and continue whisking until the mixture has thickened enough to coat a wooden spoon, 7 to 10 minutes.

Remove the mixture from the heat, mix in the butter a few pieces at a time, making sure each addition is fully incorporated before adding the next.

Stir in 2 tablespoons of the peach schnapps and set the curd aside to cool to room temperature. (The curd can be made ahead and kept in an airtight container in the refrigerator for several days; stir until smooth before using).

To make the soaking syrup, in a saucepan combine the orange juice, Cointreau, vanilla bean, 1 teaspoon of the peach extract, and ¼ cup of the sugar. Bring to a boil, stirring to dissolve sugar. Cook for 5 minutes (this allows alcohol to evaporate), then remove from the heat and let cool to room temperature. Remove and reserve the vanilla bean. (Can be made a day ahead and kept in a jar in the refrigerator.)

To make the zabaglione, combine the remaining 3 egg yolks, the remaining 2 tablespoons of sugar, the remaining ¼ cup of

Chantilly Cream (page 183), for serving

Toasted sliced almonds, for serving

Strips of orange zest, for serving

Twelve to eighteen 3- to 4-ounce glass serving dishes

Handheld electric mixer

Pastry bag and large round tip

schnapps, and the remaining teaspoon of peach extract in a medium heatproof bowl and set over a saucepan of simmering water. Whisk constantly for 8 to 10 minutes, or until the mixture reaches a custard consistency, coating the back of a wooden spoon. Remove the zabaglione from the heat and continue whisking as the mixture cools and thickens further, 2 to 3 more minutes. Let cool to room temperature, then wrap tightly and refrigerate until chilled, about 30 minutes. If you want to make the zabaglione ahead (from several hours to 1 day), press the plastic to the surface of the custard to prevent it from forming a skin.

When you are ready to assemble the tiramisu, slice and coarsely chop the peaches, put them in a bowl, and squeeze the lemon half over top. Stir gently to coat the peaches with the lemon juice. Set aside.

Drain any watery liquid from the top of the mascarpone. Put the mascarpone in a large mixing bowl and give it a good stir to soften. Scrape the seeds from the reserved vanilla bean into the mascarpone and stir to combine. Add the orange zest and stir until creamy, then use a flexible rubber spatula to fold in the limoncello curd until just combined. Add the zabaglione in thirds, folding gently with a flexible spatula to combine.

In a separate large bowl, whip the heavy cream to stiff peaks, then gradually add the mascarpone-zabaglione mixture to the whipped cream a little at a time, folding gently to combine.

Cut the ladyfingers into pieces as needed to fit the serving dishes you are using (you may need short little pieces for the bottom and middle layers, but longer pieces to stand up around the sides of the dishes). Dip the cookies in the soaking liquid, letting them absorb some of the liquid but not so much that they go soggy—al dente toward the center is good.

Lay a soaked ladyfinger flat in the bottom of each serving dish, then stand a few cookie pieces on end around the inside of the dish (leave space between them; you want the velvety cream to peek through). Use a pastry bag to pipe in a layer of the mascarpone-zabaglione-cream mixture (you can spoon it in instead, but piping is much neater and easier). Top with a layer of peaches (reserve enough peaches to top the tiramisu). Continue layering as needed, depending on the size and shape of your serving dishes.

Refrigerate, covered, for at least 6 hours or overnight. Let sit at room temperature 30 minutes before serving. Serve topped with Chantilly cream, a peach slice, a few almonds, and a twist of orange rind.

Pineapple Kabobs with
Coconut–Key Lime
Cream & Dulce de
Leche Dunk

page {164}

Tutti Frutti BBQ

love using the grill to make desserts, especially once the heat and humidity of summertime take hold and it's just too damn hot even to think about turning on the oven to bake anything. Plus, the summer season brings so many delicious fruits that grill up beautifully in just a few moments—slabs of watermelon, halved peaches and apricots, whole figs, skewered strawberries or cubes of cantaloupe, cracked fresh coconut—and are wonderful with a scoop of vanilla ice cream, cool creamy vanilla custard, Chantilly cream, etc. Following are a few of my special favorites, from simple grilled plums with crème fraîche to a few more complex concoctions.

Grilled Plums with Basil-White Balsamic Syrup and Lemony Crème Fraîche

Simple to prepare, this is a lovely, sophisticated, not-so-sweet treat for mid to late summer, when plums are in their prime.

•MAKES 1 DOZEN•

LEMONY CRÈME FRAÎCHE

1 cup crème fraîche

2 teaspoons freshly grated lemon zest from 1 lemon

2 tablespoons freshly squeezed lemon juice from 1 lemon

1 to 2 teaspoons honey, optional

BASIL-WHITE BALSAMIC SYRUP

½ cup (packed) fresh basil leaves, thinly sliced into ribbons, plus more for garnish

1 cup white balsamic vinegar

¼ cup granulated sugar

GRILLED PLUMS

½ cup apricot jam

½ teaspoon cinnamon

12 firm, ripe plums, halved

equipment

Twenty-four small bamboo skewers

To make the lemony crème fraîche, whisk together the crème fraîche, lemon zest, and lemon juice in a small mixing bowl. Keep refrigerated in an airtight container until ready to use, up to 3 days.

To make the syrup, put the basil in a medium heatproof bowl and set aside.

Bring the vinegar and sugar to a boil in a small, heavy-bottom saucepan over medium-high heat. Cook, stirring occasionally, for 5 to 10 minutes, or until the sugar is dissolved and the liquid is reduced by half.

Pour the hot syrup over the basil and let cool to room temperature, 15 to 30 minutes.

Pour the cooled syrup through a small strainer into a jar or sealable storage container. Discard the strained basil. Cover until ready to use. (The syrup can be kept in an airtight container in the refrigerator for several days.)

To cook the plums, soak 24 small bamboo skewers in water for at least 15 minutes. Heat the grill to medium and brush the grill rack with oil.

Heat the jam in a small saucepan over low heat until melted, 2 to 3 minutes. Remove from heat and stir in the cinnamon.

Halve and pit the plums. To double-skewer the plum halves in pairs, first thread one skewer through the fruit just to one side of the hollow left by the pit. Add second plum half to the skewer. Then thread a second skewer through both plum halves just to the other side of the hollow from the pit (this will help keep the plums flat on the grill and prevent them from sliding around on the skewers). Brush the cut sides of the plums with the jam mixture.

Grill the plums until nicely marked and just beginning to soften, about 2 minutes per side. (Try to turn just once; flipping repeatedly will beat up the fruit.)

Serve at room temperature. Slide each pair of plum halves off the skewers and onto individual serving dishes. Fill the hollow of each plum with lemony crème fraîche, overfilling slightly so that the creamy sauce drips over the sides of the fruit and pools a little on the plate. Drizzle all over with the basil–white balsamic syrup, garnish with snipped basil, and serve with little pitchers of additional crème fraîche and syrup. Alternatively, leave the plums on the skewers, garnish with fresh basil, and serve on a large platter with pitchers of crème fraîche and balsamic syrup alongside.

Pineapple Kabobs with Coconut–Key Lime Cream and Dulce de Leche Dunk

Like a (virgin) piña colada on a stick! (Did you know that "colada" means sword? How perfect is that?) This amazing combination of flavors transports me straight to the tropics. It is a big crowd-pleaser and a fantastic party treat.

• MAKES 18 •

Coconut–Key Lime Cream
(page 165)

1 pineapple

¼ cup coconut syrup reserved
from Coconut–Key Lime Cream

2 tablespoons marmalade

1 to 2 tablespoons honey, optional

½ teaspoon cinnamon

Dulce de Leche Dunk (page 165)

½ cup sweetened coconut flakes,
lightly toasted

Lime zest

Mint sprigs

equipment

Eighteen small bamboo skewers

Soak the skewers in water for at least 30 minutes. Preheat the grill to medium.

Make the Coconut–Key Lime Cream.

Cut off the top and bottom of the pineapple. Cut away the peel, then cut the pineapple in half lengthwise. Core both halves of the pineapple, then cut each half lengthwise into 9 rectangular 1-inch-thick slices, for a total of 18 slices. Thread each pineapple slice lengthwise onto a soaked skewer.

Combine the leftover coconut syrup from the Coconut–Key Lime Cream and marmalade in a small saucepan and cook over low heat until melted, 3 to 5 minutes, whisking to combine. Remove the saucepan from the heat and whisk in the honey, then the cinnamon. Let the glaze cool slightly, then use a basting brush to coat the pineapple skewers on both sides.

Lightly oil the grill and cook the pineapple skewers until nicely marked and caramelized, turning once, 3 to 5 minutes per side. Resist the urge to fiddle with them—just turn them once and they will have one clean set of grill marks per side rather than looking like they got run over by an ATV.

Garnish with toasted coconut, lime zest, and mint sprigs and serve with the Dulce de Leche Dunk and Coconut–Key Lime Cream.

Coconut–Key Lime Cream *Makes about 2 cups*

The richness of coconut plus the brightness of lime equals sheer bliss. Don't even think about trying this with coconut milk or "light" coconut cream—it won't thicken (believe me, I've tried!)

One 15-ounce can coconut cream (*not coconut milk!*), chilled several hours or overnight

1 to 2 teaspoons freshly squeezed lime juice, preferably from Key limes

1 to 2 teaspoons freshly grated lime zest, preferably from Key limes

equipment

Handheld electric mixer

Set a fine mesh sieve over a bowl and pour in the entire can of coconut cream. Transfer the solids to a mixing bowl. Pour off and reserve ¼ cup of the coconut syrup (for use in the Pineapple Kabobs, page 164), and the remaining syrup to the mixing bowl with the coconut solids.

Whip with a handheld electric mixer, using upward and back-and-forth motions to work a lot of air into the coconut cream. It will take as long as 10 minutes to become fluffy, thick, and creamy. Add lime juice and zest and mix to combine. Keep refrigerated until ready to use (the cream rapidly softens at room temperature). The cream can be kept in an airtight container in the refrigerator for a week.

Dulce de Leche Dunk *Makes about 1 cup*

For use as a dip (as for the pineapple kabobs) or pouring sauce, go with the shorter cooking time. The longer times will yield a dulche de leche that is a very thick, pudding-like consistency that's incredibly delicious but too thick to use as a dip or pouring sauce. But if you cook it a bit too long, or if it thickens after it's done (it's a great make-ahead dish as it keeps well for a long time in the fridge, but it does tend to thicken even more when chilled)—not to worry. Gently rewarm it in a heatproof bowl over a saucepan of gently simmering water, and whisk in warm whole milk a little at a time until you get the desired consistency.

One 14-ounce can sweetened condensed milk

Fill a large deep soup pot with enough water to cover the can by a depth of at least 2 inches. Peel the paper label off of the can. Set the unopened can in the pot of water and bring the water to a boil over high heat. Lower the heat, cover, and simmer for at least 3 and up to 4 hours (cooking for the longer time gets you a darker, richer, thicker dulce de leche). Add boiling water as needed to maintain a minimum 2-inch depth over the top of the can. If you hear the can gently rattling against the pot, you've got a nice simmer going. If it sounds more like clanking or knocking, it's boiling a bit too hard and you need to lower the heat or set the pot on a flame tamer.

Use a pair of long-handled tongs to lift the can out of the water. Let cool for at least 1 hour before opening.

Store for up to a month in an airtight glass jar in the refrigerator. Rewarm very gently, by standing the jar in a bowl of hot water. Or transfer to a heatproof bowl and warm over simmering water, whisking in a little whole milk to thin as needed.

Grilled Banana S'mores

Bananas caramelize beautifully on the grill. Sandwich them on cinnamon pizzelle with ganache and a drizzling of homemade marshmallow cream for a fun and super-yummy twist on an old fave. Need to keep it simpler? Get some ice cream and toppings and go for grilled banana splits!

•MAKES ABOUT 2 DOZEN•

6 firm bananas (ripe, but just barely)

2 tablespoons lemon juice

½ cup honey

3 to 4 tablespoons cinnamon

24 Cinnamon Pizzelle (page 169), or Pizzette rounds (from Fig Pizzette, page 5)

Marshmallow Cream (page 186)

Ganache (page 181)

Keeping the bananas unpeeled, slice them in half lengthwise and then crosswise.

Set the bananas cut-side up on a rimmed baking sheet. Sprinkle on the lemon juice, drizzle with the honey, then dust with the cinnamon. Let sit at room temperature.

Meanwhile, preheat the grill to medium.

Grill the bananas, cut-side down, for 2 minutes or until nicely marked. Turn and cook about 5 more minutes, or until the skin easily pulls away from the fruit.

To assemble the s'mores, slather a pizzelle wafer with ganache, add a piece of grilled banana and some marshmallow sauce, and top with a second pizzelle wafer.

Cinnamon Pizzelle *Makes about 4 dozen pizzelle*

Crispy and light, so pretty with their embossed patterning, pizzelle are traditional Italian wafers made from a very simple, standard batter—just eggs, butter, flour, baking powder, sugar, and a little salt. This variation adds cinnamon to the mix.

3½ cups all-purpose flour

4 teaspoons baking powder

¼ teaspoon fine sea salt

2 teaspoons cinnamon

8 ounces (2 sticks) butter, melted and slightly cooled

1½ cups granulated sugar

6 large eggs

1 teaspoon vanilla extract

equipment

Nonstick electric pizzelle press that makes 4-inch pizzelle and has an indicator light

Handheld electric mixer

Preheat the pizzelle iron.

Sift together the flour, baking powder, salt, and cinnamon in a medium bowl.

In a separate large bowl, use a handheld electric mixer to beat together the butter and sugar. Beat in the eggs one at a time. Stir in the vanilla.

Add the flour mixture to the butter mixture, mixing by hand just until blended. Do not overmix.

Scoop rounded tablespoons of the dough and form into about 4 dozen balls. Working in batches, set 1 ball onto each circle on the press, placing very slightly off-center toward the back of the machine.

Bake until light golden brown, 30 to 60 seconds. Transfer to cutting board and, while the wafers are still warm and pliable, use scissors or the tip of a small sharp knife to trim off any excess from the edges. Cool on a wire rack. Store in an airtight container for up to 1 week.

> tip: For turning out pizzelle like a nonna, have a sidekick to help trim down the pizzelles as they come off the press, when still warm and pliable; it can take a couple of tries to get the temperature and amount of batter just right—don't get discouraged if the first round or two often get tossed (or snacked on).

Grilled Cherry-Rosemary Galettini

Rustic cherry tarts from the grill make a beautiful finish to a summer dinner party. They are also great as a sweet-savory little something with wine or cocktails. Note that to bake the tarts you will need a grill that has a lid and a reliable temperature gauge as well as a grill-proof baking stone.

PASTRY

2½ cups all-purpose flour

¾ teaspoon fine sea salt

8 ounces (2 sticks) cold unsalted butter, cut into ½-inch cubes

1 teaspoon finely chopped fresh rosemary

⅓ cup ice water, plus more as needed

FILLING

1 pound fresh dark sweet cherries, pitted and halved (about 2 cups)

2 tablespoons granulated sugar

2 teaspoons finely chopped fresh rosemary

6 ounces chèvre, at room temperature

Coarse sugar, for sprinkling

equipment

Food processor

3-inch round cutter, or a glass, can, or bowl with an opening of that diameter

Gas grill with thermometer

Grill-proof pizza or baking stone

Large pizza peel

To make the pastry dough, combine the flour, salt, and butter in the bowl of a food processor fitted with the standard blade. Pulse until the mixture resembles very coarse cornmeal, 8 to 10 times. Add the rosemary and ⅓ cup of the ice water, then pulse the machine a few times. Add more ice water 1 tablespoon at a time, pulsing only enough to uniformly combine the ingredients—just until the mixture begins to gather together, but not long enough to allow it to form a ball.

Turn the dough out onto a large sheet of parchment or wax paper. Lightly pat the pieces together through the paper. Split the dough into 2 equal portions, pat each into a thick flat disk, wrap tightly, and refrigerate until well chilled, at least 2 hours.

To prepare the cherry filling, combine the cherries (with their accumulated juice) and the granulated sugar in a large bowl and mix well. Heat a large heavy skillet over medium-high heat on the stove (or on the grill if you like!). Pour the cherries and juice into the skillet and stir well. The juice will immediately begin to bubble and give off a caramel aroma. Continue cooking, stirring once or twice, until the cherry juice has reduced by about half and become syrupy, about 5 minutes. Remove the skillet from the heat and stir in the remaining 2 teaspoons rosemary.

To assemble and cook the first dozen galettini, preheat a grill with a pizza or baking stone to 425°F. Line a large pizza peel with a sheet of parchment paper.

On a smooth, lightly floured work surface, roll out 1 of the chilled disks of dough to an even thickness of no more than ¼ inch. Use a 3-inch round cutter to cut out 12 circles of dough. Arrange the

dough circles on the parchment-lined pizza peel, spacing about 1 inch apart. (Or wrap tightly in plastic and refrigerate for up to 2 days; or double-wrap and freeze for up to 1 month.)

Spread a generous teaspoon of chèvre on each of the dough rounds, then top each with four cherry halves, cut side down. Turn up the edges of each dough round to make a rim around the cherries. Sprinkle with half of the coarse sugar.

Check that the grill temperature is at least 425°F (a little hotter won't hurt, since the temperature tends to drop every time you open the lid). Turn off the flame under the baking stone (leave the flame on for the other half of the grill). As quickly as possible, open the grill lid and slide the parchment onto the baking stone. Close the lid immediately. Bake the galettini for 15 minutes, leaving the lid closed and monitoring the grill temperature; if it drops below 350°F, relight the flame under the stone and set it to low.

While the first dozen galettini bake, assemble the second dozen on a second sheet of parchment paper.

After 15 minutes, the first dozen galettini should be crispy and browned around the edges. (If not, give them a few more minutes.) To get them off the grill, slide the edge of the pizza peel under a corner of the parchment paper. The parchment won't be hot, so you can grasp the corner of the paper to pull it onto the peel. Quickly close the grill lid.

Set the first dozen galettini aside to cool. Slide the second dozen, on their sheet of parchment paper, onto the stone and repeat the cooking process.

Serve at room temperature.

Sweet Salvation—Quick Fixes and Finesses

I know baking can be intimidating sometimes, especially when things don't come out perfect! Just try and remember that everyone messes up now and then. A little camouflage often does the trick: try adding some whipped cream, a little powdered sugar, or maybe a dusting of cocoa powder or a sprinkling of chopped nuts or shaved chocolate to cover a mistake. Also, there are plenty of drizzles, creams, and glazes in my Basics section that can make any dessert gone awry look like confection perfection (I say just about everything benefits from a little ganache!). If a cake doesn't set up right, don't worry—you'll figure out what went wrong next time. Meantime, cube that baby up and layer it with one of my creams or custards or frostings, maybe some fruit as well, and make a trifle— which, it's worth noting, is also known as parfait (as in French for perfect). Use your imagination, mix things up to find your own magical combo that makes you a Goddess of Sweets, too!

{basics}

Basic Pastry—Single Crust

2½ cups all-purpose flour

½ teaspoon fine sea salt

8 ounces (2 sticks) cold unsalted butter, cut into ½-inch cubes

⅓ cup ice water, plus more if needed

equipment

Food processor

Combine the flour and salt in the bowl of a food processor fitted with the standard blade and pulse to combine. Add the butter and pulse until the mixture resembles very coarse cornmeal (just a few 1-second pulses). Add ⅓ cup ice water, then pulse the machine a few more times. Add more ice water, 1 teaspoon at a time, pulsing only enough to combine the ingredients—just until the mixture begins to gather together, but not long enough to allow it to form a ball.

Turn the dough out onto a large sheet of wax paper. Lightly pat the pieces together through the paper. Split the dough into 2 equal portions, pat each into a thick flat disk, wrap tightly, and refrigerate until well chilled, at least 2 hours, before rolling out and cutting. (Before or after rolling and cutting, the dough can be tightly wrapped and refrigerated overnight or double-wrapped and frozen for 1 month. If you know what size and/or shape you are going to be using, you can go a step further and cut them as well, layer with parchment or wax paper, then double wrap and freeze.)

Basic Pastry—Double Crust/Lattice Top

3⅓ cups all-purpose flour

¾ teaspoon fine sea salt

11 ounces (2⅔ sticks) cold unsalted butter, cut into ½-inch cubes

⅓ cup ice water, plus more if needed

equipment

Food processor

Combine the flour and salt in the bowl of a food processor fitted with the standard blade and pulse to combine. Add the butter and pulse until the mixture resembles very coarse cornmeal (just a few 1-second pulses). Add ⅓ cup ice water, then pulse the machine a few more times. Add more ice water, 1 teaspoon at a time, pulsing only enough to combine the ingredients—just until the mixture begins to gather together, but not long enough to allow it to form a ball.

Turn the dough out onto a large sheet of wax paper. Lightly pat the pieces together through the paper. Split the dough into 2 equal portions, pat each into a thick flat disk, wrap tightly, and refrigerate until well chilled, at least 2 hours, before rolling out and cutting. (Before or after rolling and cutting, the dough can be tightly wrapped and refrigerated overnight or double-wrapped and frozen for 1 month. If you know what size and/or shape you are going to be using, you can go a step further and cut them as well, layer with parchment or wax paper, then double wrap and freeze.)

Rustica Pastry

2¼ cups flour

⅓ cup confectioners' sugar

½ teaspoon fine sea salt

7 ounces (1¾ sticks) cold unsalted butter, cut into ¼-inch cubes

1 teaspoon finely grated orange zest

2 large egg yolks (1 white reserved for egg wash)

1 teaspoon vanilla extract

½ teaspoon orange extract

2 tablespoons cold water, plus more as needed

equipment

Food processor

Combine the flour, sugar, salt, butter, and orange zest in the bowl of a food processor fitted with a standard blade. Pulse 8 to 10 times, or just until the mixture looks like a coarse cornmeal with some pea-sized clumps of butter. Add the egg yolks, vanilla and orange extracts, and 2 tablespoons of the cold water and pulse a few more times to combine. Add more water, a teaspoon at a time, and continue pulsing just until the dough begins to form large lumps.

Pat the dough into 2 disks, wrap it tightly, and chill it in the refrigerator for 45 minutes to 1 hour. (The dough can be made ahead and kept in the refrigerator overnight or up to 3 days before using. If it chills for more than an hour, it will be very stiff; let sit at room temperature for about 20 minutes to soften.)

Simple Syrup

2 cups raw sugar, such as turbinado or demerara

Combine the sugar with 1 cup water in a small heavy-bottom saucepan and bring the mixture to a boil over medium-high heat. Cook, stirring occasionally, until the sugar is completely dissolved and the syrup is clear, about 5 minutes.

Use immediately or keep in an airtight container in the refrigerator.

Orange Blossom Syrup

1½ cups granulated sugar

1 tablespoon lemon juice

2 tablespoons *mazaher* (orange blossom water)

Combine the sugar and ¾ cup water in a medium heavy-bottom saucepan and cook over medium-high heat for a few minutes, stirring constantly, until the sugar is dissolved and the liquid starts to boil. Add the lemon juice and lower the heat to a simmer and continue cooking 10 more minutes. (It may seem thin, but it will thicken up as it cools. It needs to be pourable, so don't overcook. If you do let it get too thick, you'll need to rewarm it and add a little more water to thin it down.) Take the saucepan off the heat, stir in the *mazaher*, pour the syrup into a heatproof container, and cool completely. Cover and reserve at room temperature. (Can be made the day before and kept at room temperature.)

Caramel Drizzle

1 cup granulated sugar

6 tablespoons unsalted butter

½ cup heavy cream

1 teaspoon vanilla extract

Pinch fine sea salt

Heat the sugar in a medium saucepan over medium-high heat, whisking constantly until the sugar melts and darkens to a pale amber color, 3 to 5 minutes.

Take the pan off the heat and add the butter all at once (the sugar will be bubbly, so be careful) and continue whisking until the butter is melted and the mixture is smooth, about 1 minute. Carefully add the cream, vanilla, and salt, whisking until smooth and fully incorporated, about 1 more minute. Let the caramel cool about 10 minutes (it will continue to thicken as it cools), then transfer to a jar; or cool completely and pour into a small squeeze bottle.

This can be made ahead and stored in an airtight jar in the refrigerator for weeks. Before serving, reheat gently (by transferring to a saucepan and warming over low heat, stirring occasionally; or by transferring to a bowl and microwaving at half power in 15-second intervals, stirring between each interval) until warmed through. If you keep the caramel in a squeeze bottle, the best way to rewarm it is to stand the squeeze bottle in a bowl of hot water for several minutes.

Variation: Sea-salted Caramel Drizzle

Instead of the pinch of fine sea salt, use ½ teaspoon fleur de sel or other sweet, flaky sea salt.

Ganache

8 ounces bittersweet or semisweet chocolate, chopped

¼ cup heavy cream

2 tablespoons unsalted butter

Combine the chocolate, cream, and butter in a small heatproof bowl. Set the bowl over a saucepan of barely simmering water. Cook, stirring occasionally, until the chocolate is melted and the mixture is very smooth.

Let the ganache cool to room temperature before using.

Dark Chocolate Glaze

MAKES 2 CUPS

1 cup heavy cream

2 tablespoons simple syrup (page 179)

8 ounces bittersweet chocolate (60% cacao), chopped

2 tablespoons unsalted butter, at room temperature

Combine the cream and the simple syrup in a medium saucepan and bring to a simmer over medium heat. Remove the pan from the heat and immediately add the chocolate. Let stand 5 minutes, then stir until silky smooth. Add the butter and stir until melted and incorporated. Let the glaze cool until it is room temperature but still pourable.

Raspberry Drizzle

12 ounces fresh raspberries, or one 12-ounce bag frozen raspberries, thawed

1 cup granulated sugar

¼ cup Chambord, Heering, or other berry or cherry liqueur

1 tablespoon cornstarch

Combine the berries, sugar, and liqueur in a small saucepan, bring to a boil over medium-high heat, then turn the heat down and simmer 20 minutes, stirring occasionally to break up the fruit and dissolve the sugar.

Set a fine-mesh sieve over a bowl. Pour the sauce through the sieve, pressing to release the fruit pulp and juices into the bowl. Pour the contents of the bowl back into the saucepan (discard the seeds left behind in the sieve). Return the syrup to a simmer, then turn the heat to very low. Dissolve the cornstarch in 1 tablespoon water, mixing until very smooth. Gradually stir the slurry into the pan. Cook, stirring constantly, over very low heat, until the sauce begins to thicken, 2 to 3 minutes. Take the pan off the heat and let the sauce cool completely to room temperature (it will continue to thicken as it cools). Keep in an airtight container in the refrigerator for up to a week.

White Chocolate Drizzle

¾ cup white chocolate chips

¼ cup heavy cream

1 teaspoon vanilla extract

Combine the white chocolate chips and the cream in a small heatproof bowl and set over a small saucepan of barely simmering water. Cook, stirring frequently, until the white chocolate is melted and the mixture is very smooth. Take the pan off the heat and add vanilla, stirring well to incorporate. Transfer to a squeeze bottle.

Keep in the refrigerator for up to 1 week. Bring to room temperature before using (you can stand the squeeze bottle in a bowl of hot water for 1 to 2 minutes to soften back to a squirtable consistency).

Lemon Curd

1 large egg

1 large egg yolk

6 tablespoons granulated sugar

¼ cup freshly squeezed lemon juice

2 tablespoons unsalted butter, at room temperature

½ teaspoon finely grated lemon zest

Whisk together the eggs, sugar, and lemon juice in a heatproof bowl and set over a saucepan of simmering water. Use a wooden spoon to stir the curd continuously until it thickens enough to coat the back of the spoon, about 9 minutes.

Strain the lemon curd through a mesh sieve. Stir in the butter, mixing until the butter is completely melted and uniformly incorporated. Mix in the lemon zest. Cover with plastic wrap (lightly pressing the wrap to the surface of the curd to prevent a skin from forming) and chill thoroughly, about 1 hour. The lemon curd can be transferred to an airtight jar and kept refrigerated for weeks; it also freezes well.

Chantilly Cream

MAKES ABOUT 2 CUPS

1 cup cold heavy cream

Seeds from ½ vanilla bean, or 1 teaspoon vanilla extract

1 tablespoon confectioners' sugar, optional

Combine the cream, vanilla, and sugar in a large bowl and whip to soft peaks.

Chocolate Hazelnut Cream

MAKES 2 CUPS

1 cup Nutella chocolate hazelnut spread

6 tablespoons semisweet chocolate chips

¾ cup cold heavy cream

equipment

Electric mixer

Combine the Nutella and the chocolate in a medium heatproof bowl and set over a small saucepan of barely simmering water. Cook for about 5 minutes or until the ingredients are completely melted and incorporated, stirring almost constantly with a whisk or a heatproof flexible spatula and frequently scraping down the sides of the bowl. The mixture will be very smooth and silky. Set aside to cool to room temperature, 20 to 30 minutes.

In a large bowl, whip the cream to stiff peaks with an electric mixer. Add the cooled chocolate mixture and whip with the mixer until well combined.

Cover with plastic wrap and refrigerate until ready to use. Soften at room temperature for 15 to 20 minutes before spreading or piping.

Peanut Butter Buttercream

MAKES ABOUT 2 CUPS

3 large egg whites

¾ cup granulated sugar

½ teaspoon vanilla extract

6 tablespoons unsalted butter, cut into tablespoons and softened

⅓ cup creamy, unsweetened natural peanut butter

Pinch fine sea salt (omit if peanut butter contains salt)

equipment

Handheld electric mixer

Candy thermometer

Stand mixer

Combine the egg whites and granulated sugar in a large heatproof mixing bowl, set the bowl over a large saucepan of steadily simmering water, and beat constantly with a handheld electric mixer for 7 to 10 minutes, or until the mixture becomes very thick and satiny and reaches 160°F on a candy thermometer.

Transfer the meringue to the bowl of a stand mixer fitted with a whisk attachment and beat at medium speed until cool, stiff, and very shiny, about 10 minutes (the bowl should be quite cool to the touch). Beat in the vanilla, then turn the mixer speed to medium-low and add the softened butter, 1 tablespoon at a time, alternating with tablespoons of the peanut butter and mixing until each addition is incorporated.

Cover and chill the buttercream for 1 hour or up to 3 days. Before using, bring to room temperature, then rewhip with the electric mixer until fluffy, 2 to 5 minutes. The buttercream also freezes beautifully; thaw overnight at room temperature, then rewhip until fluffy, about 5 minutes.

Marshmallow Cream

1 cup granulated sugar

1 cup water

3 large egg whites (fresh, or thawed frozen, but NOT pasteurized)

¼ teaspoon vanilla extract

equipment

Candy thermometer

Electric mixer

Combine the sugar and water in a small saucepan and set over medium-high heat. Bring to a boil and continue cooking, stirring occasionally with a wooden spoon, for about 5 minutes, or until the mixture registers 245 to 250°F on a candy thermometer.

While the syrup is cooking, beat the egg whites to stiff peaks with an electric mixer.

With the mixer running on low, gradually (and carefully!) add the hot syrup to the whipped egg whites, pouring in a thin steady stream. Add the vanilla, turn the mixer to high speed, and whip the mixture until cool and glossy (and marshmallowy!), about 10 minutes.

Transfer to a squeeze bottle or dollop with a spoon onto s'mores, ice cream sundaes, etc.

Keep in a jar in the refrigerator for up to a week.

(above) The Pierri Clan
(right) The Wakile Clan.

Acknowledgments

Love of home and family, joy in all things "homemade," and pride in workmanship—for all of these precious gifts I have my parents, Anthony and Maria Pierri, to thank.

I am so grateful to my in-laws, Joseph and Malake Wakile, for sharing with me their traditions and customs that have enriched our lives and will, God willing, be passed along for generations to come.

To my sweethearts, Rich, Victoria, and Joseph, thank you for your love and support—and your patience! I promise I will get back to cooking proper dinners now.

To my sister and first best friend, Rosie—I love you. Thank you for always being there!

And to the rest of my wonderful family—all of you pictured in these two photos—thank you! I love you with all of my heart.

To all of my dear friends who have called and waited patiently for me to be available to chat or to go to lunch or just to take a walk together, thank you! I love you all for understanding how important this project has been to me and I so appreciate you!

Thanks to everyone at St, Martin's Press, especially: John Murphy, for believing in me and wanting to see my recipes in print; Michael Flamini, my editor and friend, whom I will never tire of talking to about our shared love of food; and Vicki Lame, for being so helpful throughout the editorial and production process.

Thanks to my agent, Frank Weimann, for making it all happen; to Bravo TV and NBC Universal; to Sirens Media; and to all of the viewers and "Housewives" fans who encouraged me to write this book.

Miriam Harris, my cowriter, captured my voice better than I ever thought possible, and taught me the importance of writing everything down. Through this process I gained a dear friend (who now knows my thoughts before I even speak them). Thank you!

Robin Wunsh Barron, my publicist, my organizer, and so much more— thank you for keeping me on schedule.

To my "GlamBoyz" for making me look, well, glam: George Miguel (makeup) and Julius Michael (hair). Julius, my dear friend, thank you for taking care of more than just my hair!

For photography and styling, thanks to Andrei Jackamets and Gigi Alterio, and also to Villeroy Boch, for loaning beautiful dishware, and to Abbey and Thomas Kober, for graciously opening up their home, Abbey Farm, for my cover shoot.

To the many talented cooks and chefs who have influenced me along my path, thank you for your passion and inspiration.

I thank God—through Him everything has been possible—for my incredible journey thus far and for bringing into my life the people who have guided me to this path.

About the Author

Kathy Wakile is the one and only dessert expert on Bravo TV's *The Real Housewives of New Jersey* and has used her reality TV platform to help raise awareness for both the National Brain Tumor Society and the Children's Brain Tumor Foundation. Her dessert line, called Dolci della Dea, is soon to be in retail venues nationwide. Kathy regularly serves as an Honorary Professor at the L'Ecole Culinaire, an ACCSC-accredited culinary school that offers degree and diploma programs, sharing her passion and knowledge of culinary trends, and her unique experience bringing personally developed food products to market. She lives in Wayne, New Jersey, with her husband, Rich, and their children, Victoria and Joseph.

Index

A

ackawi cheese, 106
Almond Joy, 75
almonds, 27
Almond Joyous Cheesecake
    Cuties, 60–62
Almond Topping, 60–62
Apricot-Almond Filling, 108
Amalfi Coast, 155
Amaretto, 31, 108
amuse-bouche, 7
antipasti, 4
Apollo brand #7 phyllo pastry
    sheets, 37–39
apples, xv–xvi, 64
    Apple Crumblekins, xvi, 14–17, 19
    Apple Filling, 16, 19, 21, 23–24
    Apple Ricotta Zeppolini, xvi,
        15, 18
    Caramel Apple Ravioli, xvi, 15,
        22–25
    in fall, 1, 14–25
    Petite Apple Pies, xvi, 15, 19–21
apricots, 2, 161
    Apricot-Almond Filling, 108
    Doves' Nests, 105, 108, 125
    Pistachio-Apricot Mezzelune,
        33–35, 49
artisanal donuts, 97
asparagus frittatas, 65
Atlantic City, N.J., 157
attar, 105

B

babycakes
    Chocolate Babycakes, 49, 74,
        76–78, 82
    Pumpkin Spice Babycakes, 42–45

Baci candy, 101
baking powder, 169
baklawa, Pignoli Baklawa Bites,
    36–39, 49, 125
balsamic vinegar
    Basil-White Balsamic Syrup,
        162–63
    Grilled Plums with Basil-White
        Balsamic Syrup & Lemony
        Crème Fraîche, 161–63
banana bread, 73
bananas
    Bananas Foster Cream Puffs, 102
    Grilled Banana S'mores, 167–69
    Hound Dogs, 72–73
Barbara, Saint, 119
barbecues, xiii, 1, 127
    see also grilled desserts
bars, xvi, 70, 75
    Fresh Fig Pizzette Bar, 2, 5–6
basics, 173, 175–86
    Basic Pastry-Double Crust/Lat-
        tice Top, 19–21, 177
    Basic Pastry-Single Crust, 9–10,
        176
    Caramel Drizzle, 15, 24, 45, 102,
        180
    Chantilly Cream, 16, 58, 100,
        151–52, 153–54, 155–56,
        158–59, 161, 183
    Chocolate Hazelnut Cream,
        76–77, 184
    Dark Chocolate Glaze, 70–71,
        97, 116, 181
    Ganache, 61–62, 167, 181
    Lemon Curd, 56, 98, 155–56,
        183
    Marshmallow Cream, 40, 46–48,
        72–73, 167, 186

Orange Blossom Syrup, 5, 7–8,
    37–39, 106, 108, 109, 110,
    179
Peanut Butter Buttercream,
    66–67, 70, 72–73, 82, 185
Raspberry Drizzle, 55, 68–69,
    81, 182
Rustica Pastry, 5, 11, 33–35, 120,
    178
Sea-salted Caramel Drizzle,
    28–29, 180
Simple Syrup, 179, 181
White Chocolate Drizzle, 68–69,
    113, 182
basil
    Basil-White Balsamic Syrup,
        162–63
    Grilled Plums with Basil-White
        Balsamic Syrup and Lemony
        Crème Fraîche, 161–63
Beach Baby Blondies, 49, 112,
    114–15
Belmar, N.J., 146
birthdays, 87
biscotti, 51, 149
bites, xv
    Chocolate-Chili Brownie Bites,
        49, 112, 117
    Pignoli Baklawa Bites, 36–39, 49,
        125
    White Chocolate Blondie Bites,
        49, 112, 113
Bitsy Brunettes, 49, 112, 116
blondies, xv, xvii
    Beach Baby Blondies, 49, 112,
        114–15
    in spring, 112–15
    White Chocolate Blondie Bites,
        49, 112, 113

blueberries, 2
    Blueberry–Pine Nut Filling, 109
    Blueberry Streusel Baby Bundts,
        49, 84–85
Blue Jays' Nests, 105, 109, 125
borsettini, Fresh Fig Borsettini, 9–10,
    49
Bottla Red, 136–37
braciole, 4
Brazil, 92
breads, 6, 65, 69, 73
breakfasts, 149
brownies, xv
    Bitsy Brunettes, 49, 112, 116
    Chocolate-Chili Brownie Bites,
        49, 112, 117
    Nutty at Heart, 82
    in spring, 112, 116–17
brunettes, Bitsy Brunettes, 49, 112,
    116
bundts
    Baby Bundts, 78–79
    Blueberry Streusel Baby Bundts,
        49, 84–85
    Chocolate-Tangerine Baby
        Bundts, 76, 78–79
    PB&J Baby Bundts, 68–69
    Pumpkin Spice Baby Bundts, 44
buns, Pumpkin Ginger Pecan Sticky
    Buns, 45, 49
Burbara (Lebanese Wheat Berry Pud-
    ding), 119, 122–23
butter, xvii, 6, 16, 37, 169
    Maple-Brown Butter Glaze, 44
    Peanut Butter Buttercream,
        66–67, 70, 72–73, 82, 185

C

Cabbage Patch dolls, 18
cakes, 76–85, 90, 173
    for birthdays, 87
    Blueberry Streusel Baby Bundts,
        49, 84–85
    Chocolate Babycakes, 49, 74,
        76–78, 82

Chocolate-Tangerine Baby
    Bundts, 76, 78–79
Chocolate Volcanoes, xvii, 80–81
Hound Dogs, 72–73
Nutter Butter Finger Cakewiches,
    70–71
Nutty at Heart, 82
PB&J Baby Bundts, 68–69
PB&J Wonder Cakewiches, 66–67
Peanut Butter Cakes, 68–69, 70
Pumpkin Spice Baby Bundts, 44
Pumpkin Spice Babycakes, 42–45
Wonder Cake, 66–67
see also cheesecakes
calzones, 75
Campania, 90, 149
candy, xvi, 70, 75, 101, 144
cannolis, 45, 90
cantaloupe, 161
Capri, xvi, 155
Capri Mia (Limoncello Tiramisu), xv,
    xvi, 155–57
caramel, 16
    Bananas Foster Cream Puffs, 102
    Caramel Apple Ravioli, xvi, 15,
        22–25
    Caramel Chocolate Walnut Tart-
        lettini, 26, 28–29, 49
    Caramel Drizzle, 15, 24, 45, 102,
        180
    Caramel Swirl, 146–47
    Sea-salted Caramel Drizzle,
        28–29, 180
    Tanned and Salty, 146–47
Cardinals' Nests, 105, 110, 125
Cedar brand, 119
Chantilly Cream, 16, 58, 100,
    151–52, 153–54, 155–56,
    158–59, 161, 183
cheesecakes
    Almond Joyous Cheesecake
        Cuties, 60–62
    Chocolate Cheesecake Cuties,
        58–59
    Classic Cheesecake Cuties, 54–55

fundamentals of, 53
    Lemon Dream Cheesecake
        Cuties, 52, 56–57
    Wakile's adolescence and, 53
    in winter, 51–62
cheeses, 2, 5, 53, 65
    Apple Ricotta Zeppolini, xvi,
        15, 18
    Cheese Filling, 9–10, 24
    Cream Cheese Pastry, 31–32
    Knafeh Nests, 105–8, 109, 110,
        125
    Mascarpone Frosting, 42–43
    Nonni Maria's Ricotta Wheat
        Easter Pies (*Pastiera Napole-
        tana*), 118–21
    Orange Mascarpone, 5–6, 7–8
    Pan-Roasted Fresh Figs with
        Infused Honey Syrup and
        Orange Mascarpone, 7–8
cherries
    Cherry-Pistachio Filling, 110
    Chocolate-Cherry Swirl, 144–45
    Chocolate-Covered Cherry,
        144–45
    Grilled Cherry-Rosemary
        Galettini, 170–72
Chicago Metallic Lift & Serve Single
    Squares Pans, 11
chiles, Chocolate-Chili Brownie
    Bites, 49, 112, 117
chocolate, 91, 173
    Beach Baby Blondies, 49, 112,
        114–15
    Bitsy Brunettes, 49, 112, 116
    Caramel Chocolate Walnut Tart-
        lettini, 26, 28–29, 49
    Chocolate Babycakes, 49, 74,
        76–78, 82
    Chocolate Cheesecake Cuties,
        58–59
    Chocolate-Cherry Swirl, 144–45
    Chocolate-Chili Brownie Bites,
        49, 112, 117
    Chocolate-Covered Cherry,

144–45
Chocolate Custard Filling, 94–95
Chocolate Custard Tartlets,
    94–95, 125
Chocolate Hazelnut Cream,
    76–77, 184
Chocolate Hazelnut Kisses, 101
Chocolate Pastry, 28–29
Chocolate-Tangerine Baby
    Bundts, 76, 78–79
Chocolate Volcanoes, xvii, 80–81
Chocolate Walnut Filling, 28–29
Cioccolato (Chocolate Tiramisu),
    xv, 125, 148, 153–54
Dark Chocolate Glaze, 70–71,
    97, 116, 181
Lime-White Chocolate Drizzle,
    114–15
Nutty at Heart, 82
power of, 75
Tangerine-White Chocolate
    Drizzle, 78–79
Tangerine-White Chocolate
    Ripple, 78–79
Wakile's childhood and, 75
White Chocolate Blondie Bites,
    49, 112, 113
White Chocolate Drizzle, 68–69,
    113, 182
in winter, 74–82
choux, *see* puff shells
Christmas, xiii, 37, 49, 51
cinnamon, 6, 16, 108
    Cinnamon Pizzelle, 167, 169
    Cinnamon Sugar, 18
    Grilled Banana S'mores, 167–69
Cioccolato (Chocolate Tiramisu), xv,
    125, 148, 153–54
Classic Cheesecake Cuties, 54–55
Classic Tiramisu (*Tradizionale*), 49,
    151–52
cocoa-cream, 58
cocoa powder, 173
coconut, 161
    Beach Baby Blondies, 49, 112,

114–15
    Coconut-Key Lime Cream,
        164–65
    Pineapple Kabobs with Coco-
        nut-Key Lime Cream and
        Dulce de Leche Dunk, 160,
        164–66
coffee, 6, 11, 84
    Espresso with a Shot (or Not),
        132–33
    Tradizionale (Classic Tiramisu), 49,
        151–52
coffeecakes
    Blueberry Streusel Baby Bundts,
        49, 84–85
    in winter, 83–85
cookies, 26, 51, 70, 94
    see also ladyfingers
coulis, 93
Cozy's Sweet Shop, 75
cream cheese, 24, 53
    Cream Cheese Pastry, 31–32
cream puffs
    Bananas Foster Cream Puffs, 102
    Chocolate Hazelnut Kisses, 101
    Pulcinelli Limoni (Little Lemon
        Chicks), 98–99
    in spring, 96–102
    Strawberry Shortcake Puffs, 100
creams, xvii, 89
    Capri Mia (Limoncello Tiramisu),
        155–57
    Chantilly Cream, 16, 58, 100,
        151–52, 153–54, 155–56,
        158–59, 161, 183
    Chocolate-Covered Cherry,
        144–45
    Chocolate Hazelnut Cream,
        76–77, 184
    Cioccolato (Chocolate Tiramisu),
        125, 148, 153–54
    Coconut-Key Lime Cream,
        164–65
    Espresso with a Shot (or Not),
        132–33

Fuzzy Navel (Peach Tiramisu),
    157–59
Grilled Banana S'mores, 167–69
Grilled Plums with Basil-White
    Balsamic Syrup and Lemony
    Crème Fraîche, 161–63
Lemon Cream Filling, 98–99
Lemony Crème Fraîche, 161–63
Marshmallow Cream, 40, 46–48,
    72–73, 167, 186
Peanut Butter Buttercream,
    66–67, 70, 72–73, 82, 185
Petite Pumpkin Pies with Toasted
    Marshmallow Topping, 40,
    46–48
Pineapple Kabobs with Coco-
    nut-Key Lime Cream and
    Dulce de Leche Dunk,
    160, 164–66
Strawberries-and-Cream,
    140–41
Tanned and Salty, 146–47
Tradizionale (Classic Tiramisu), 49,
    151–52
whipped, 100, 133, 173
crema, la, 87–95, 97
    Chocolate Custard Tartlets,
        94–95, 125
    Nonni Maria's Custard Cream,
        90–91, 94
    in spring, 87–95, 97
    Strawberry Panna Cotta, 93
    Wakile's childhood and, 89
    Zia Regina's Flan, xv, 88, 92
crème brûlée, xvi
crumbles
    Apple Crumblekins, xvi, 14–17,
        19
    Crumble Toppings, 16
crusts, 5–6, 31, 46, 54, 56, 58, 61
    Basic Pastry-Double Crust/Lat-
        tice Top, 19–21, 177
    Basic Pastry-Single Crust, 9–10,
        176
cupcakes, xvii, 97

custards, xvi–xvii, 67, 89, 161, 173
  Chocolate Custard Filling, 94–95
  Chocolate Custard Tartlets,
    94–95, 125
  Nonni Maria's Custard Cream,
    90–91, 94
  Wakile's childhood and, 89
cuties
  Almond Joyous Cheesecake
    Cuties, 60–62
  Chocolate Cheesecake Cuties,
    58–59
  Classic Cheesecake Cuties, 54–55
  Lemon Dream Cheesecake
    Cuties, 52, 56–57

D

dairy, 87, 119
desserts
  in Mediterranean region, xv
  peacemaking potential of, 125
  physical appearance of, xvii
  retro, 97
dinner parties, 51, 170
Domenico, Uncle, xiv
donuts, 97
doughs, xvii, 10, 21, 45
Doves' Nests, 105, 108, 125
drizzles, 173
  Caramel Drizzle, 15, 24, 45, 102,
    180
  Lime-White Chocolate Drizzle,
    114–15
  Raspberry Drizzle, 55, 68–69,
    81, 182
  Sea-salted Caramel Drizzle,
    28–29, 180
  Tangerine-White Chocolate
    Drizzle, 78–79
  White Chocolate Drizzle, 68–69,
    113, 182
Dulce de Leche Dunk, 164–66

E

Easter, 87

Nonni Maria's Ricotta Wheat
  Easter Pies (*Pastiera Napoletana*), 118–21
eclairs, 97
eggplants, 65
eggs, xviii, 67, 76, 87, 89, 119, 149,
  169
espresso, 125, 131
  Espresso with a Shot (or Not),
    132–33
  Tradizionale (Classic Tiramisu), 49,
    151–52

F

fall, 1–48
  apples in, 1, 14–25
  figs in, 1–13
  nuts in, 1, 26–39
  pumpkins in, 1, 40–48
feast of Saint Barbara, 119
figs, xv, 161
  in fall, 1–13
  Fig Filling, 9–10
  Figs in Baskets, 11–13, 49
  Fresh Fig *Borsettini*, 9–10, 49
  Fresh Fig Pizzette Bar, 2, 5–6
  in Mediterranean region, 1, 3–4
  Pan-Roasted Fresh Figs with
    Infused Honey Syrup and
    Orange Mascarpone, 7–8
  Wakile's childhood and, 3
  Wakile's engagement and, 4
fillings, 33–35, 44, 46, 54, 56, 58,
  61, 68, 72, 170
  Apple Filling, 16, 19, 21, 23–24
  Apricot-Almond Filling, 108
  Blueberry-Pine Nut Filling, 109
  Cheese Filling, 9–10, 24
  Cherry-Pistachio Filling, 110
  Chocolate Custard Filling, 94–95
  Chocolate Walnut Filling, 28–29
  Fig Filling, 9–10
  Lemon Cream Filling, 98–99
  Peanut Butter Buttercream,
    66–67, 70, 73–74, 82, 185

  Pecan Filling, 31–32
  Pignoli Filling, 37–38
finesses, 173
flans, Zia Regina's Flan, xvi, 88, 92
flours, xvii, 76, 81, 83, 89, 169
Forty Day Mass, 119
Fresh Fig *Borsettini*, 9–10, 49
Fresh Fig Pizzette Bar, 2, 5–6
frostings, xvii, 173
  Mascarpone Frosting, 42–43
frozen custard, xvi, 142
fruits, xvi, 8, 51, 83, 90, 93, 137,
  173
fudge, xvii, 57, 76, 94
  Nutty at Heart, 82
Fuzzy Navel (Peach Tiramisu),
  157–59

G

galettini, Grilled Cherry-Rosemary
  Galettini, 170–72
ganache, 173
  basic, 61–62, 167, 181
  Cioccolato (Chocolate Tiramisu),
    xv, 125, 148, 153–54
  Grilled Banana S'mores, 167–69
Garden State Parkway, 127
gelato, 16
  Chocolate-Covered Cherry,
    144–45
  Orange Dreamsicle, 142–43
  Strawberries-and-Cream,
    140–41
  in summer, 138–47
  Tanned and Salty, 146–47
Gelotti, 139
ginger, 108
  Pumpkin Ginger Pecan Sticky
    Buns, 45, 49
glazes, 173
  Dark Chocolate Glaze, 70–71,
    97, 116, 181
  Maple-Brown Butter Glaze, 44
gluten, avoidance of, 58, 61, 81

granita
    Bottla Red, 136–37
    Espresso with a Shot (or Not),
        132–33
    Granita *a Modo Mio* (My Way), 130
    Pink Lady, 134–35
    in summer, 128–37, 139
    Tony's Lemon Ice, 128–29, 131
grapefruits, Pink Lady, 134–35
Greeks, Greece, 4, 37
grilled desserts
    Grilled Banana S'mores, 167–69
    Grilled Cherry-Rosemary
        Galettini, 170–72
    Grilled Plums with Basil-White
        Balsamic Syrup and Lemony
        Crème Fraîche,
        161–63
    Pineapple Kabobs with Coco-
        nut-Key Lime Cream and
        Dulce de Leche Dunk, 160,
        164–66
    in summer, 160–72
Groundhog Day, 87

H

Halloween, 41
hazelnuts, 27, 74
    Chocolate Hazelnut Cream,
        76–77, 184
    Chocolate Hazelnut Kisses, 101
herbs, 93
Holiday Treat Tray, 49
holidays, xiii, xv, 1, 51
    treat tray for, 49
honey
    Infused Honey Syrup, 5–6, 7–8
    Pan-Roasted Fresh Figs with
        Infused Honey Syrup and
        Orange Mascarpone, 7–8
Hot Tamales, 75
Hound Dogs, 72–73

I

ice cream, 8, 16, 97, 141, 161, 167
    see also gelato
ice-cream makers, 130
ices, *see* granita
Infused Honey Syrup, 5–6, 7–8
Italians, Italy, 31, 37, 131, 155
    Wakile's heritage and, xiv–xv, 3,
        41, 87, 90, 92, 112, 119,
        139, 149–50
    Wakile's trips to, 87, 143–44,
        149–50
Itty Bitty Pecan Pies, 30–32, 49

J

jam, 5, 51
jellies, *see* peanut butter and jelly
Joseph, Saint, 87

K

kabobs, Pineapple Kabobs with Co-
    conut-Key Lime Cream and
    Dulce de Leche Dunk,
    160, 164–66
Kahlúa, 151
kisses, Chocolate Hazelnut Kisses,
    101
Knafeh Nests, 105–8, 109, 110, 125
Kohr's, 142

L

ladyfingers
    Cioccolato (Chocolate Tiramisu),
        xv, 125, 148, 153–54
    Tradizionale (Classic Tiramisu), 49,
        151–52
lasagna, 4
lattice tops, Basic Pastry-Double
    Crust/Lattice Top, 19–21, 177
Lebanese, Lebanon, xv, 4, 27
    Knafeh Nests, 105–8, 109, 110,
        125
    Teta Melake's Lebanese Wheat
        Berry Pudding (*Sneyniyeh* or
        Burbara), 119, 122–23
    Pignoli *Baklawa* Bites, 36–39, 49,
        125

lemonade, 157
lemons, 40, 89, 91
    Capri Mia (*Limoncello* Tiramisu), xv,
        155–57
    Grilled Plums with Basil-White
        Balsamic Syrup and
        Lemony Crème Fraîche,
        161–63
    Lemon Cream Filling, 98–99
    Lemon Curd, 56, 98, 155–56,
        183
    Lemon Dream Cheesecake
        Cuties, 52, 56–57
    Lemony Crème Fraîche, 161–63
    Pulcinelli Limoni (Little Lemon
        Chicks), 98–99
    Tony's Lemon Ice, 128–29, 131
Lent, 87
licorice, 75, 133
limes
    Beach Baby Blondies, 49, 112,
        114–15
    Coconut-Key Lime Cream,
        164–65
    Lime-White Chocolate Drizzle,
        114–15
    Pineapple Kabobs with Coco-
        nut-Key Lime Cream and
        Dulce de Leche Dunk, 160,
        164–66
Limoncello Tiramisu (*Capri Mia*), xv,
    xvi, 155–57
Little Lemon Chicks (*Pulcinelli Limo-
ni*), 98–99
Love nests
    Blue Jays' Nests, 105, 109, 125
    Cardinals' Nests, 105, 110, 125
    Doves' Nests, 105, 108, 125
    Knafeh Nests, 105–8, 109, 110,
        125
    in spring, 104–10

M

macadamia nuts, 114–15
mangos, 137

Maple-Brown Butter Glaze, 44

maple walnut ice cream, 16

marsala, 149, 153

marshmallows
    Grilled Banana S'mores, 167–69
    Marshmallow Cream, 40, 46–48,
        72–73, 167, 186
    Petite Pumpkin Pies with Toasted
        Marshmallow Topping, 40,
        46–48

mascarpone
    Mascarpone Frosting, 43
    Orange Mascarpone, 5–6, 7–8
    Pan-Roasted Fresh Figs with
        Infused Honey Syrup and
        Orange Mascarpone,
        7–8

mazaher (orange blossom water), 37,
    39, 125, 179

meatballs, 4

Mediterranean region, xv
    figs in, 1, 3–4
    Knafeh Nests and, 105–8, 109,
        110, 125
    nuts in, 1, 27
    Wakile's heritage and, 1, 4

mezzelunes (half-moons), Pis-
    tachio-Apricot Mezzelune,
    33–35, 49

milk, 6, 149
    Dulce de Leche Dunk, 164–66
    Pineapple Kabobs with Coco-
        nut-Key Lime Cream and
        Dulce de Leche Dunk,
        160, 164–66

mini bundt pans, 68–69, 78

mini muffin pans and cups, 28, 112

mini tart shells, 95

mint, Pink Lady, 134–35

mistakes, 173

Mother's Day, 119

mousses, 69

mozzarella, 106

muffin pans, 17, 19

N

New Jersey, 3–4, 41
    in summer, xvi, 127, 131, 142,
        144, 146, 157

New Orleans, LA., 102

nighttime soaps, 33

Nonni Maria's Custard Cream,
    90–91, 94

Nonni Maria's Ricotta Wheat Easter
    Pies (*Pastiera Napoletana*), 118–21

nuts, xv, 2, 5, 16, 51, 58, 74, 83,
    173
    Almond Joyous Cheesecake
        Cuties, 60–62
    Almond Topping, 60–62
    Apricot-Almond Filling, 108
    Beach Baby Blondies, 49, 112,
        114–15
    Bitsy Brunettes, 49, 112, 116
    Blueberry-Pine Nut Filling, 109
    Blue Jays' Nests, 105, 109, 125
    buttery earthy decadence of, 27
    Caramel Chocolate Walnut Tart-
        lettini, 26, 28–29, 49
    Cardinals' Nests, 105, 110, 125
    Cherry-Pistachio Filling, 110
    Chocolate Hazelnut Cream,
        76–77, 184
    Chocolate Hazelnut Kisses, 101
    Chocolate Walnut Filling, 28–29
    in fall, 1, 26–39
    Itty Bitty Pecan Pies, 30–32, 49
    in Mediterranean region, 1, 27
    Pecan Filling, 31–32
    Pignoli *Baklawa* Bites, 36–39, 49,
        125
    Pignoli Filling, 37–38
    Pistachio-Apricot Mezzelune,
        33–35, 49
    Pumpkin Ginger Pecan Sticky
        Buns, 45, 49
    Wakile's childhood and, 27
    see also peanut butter; peanut
        butter and jelly

O

orange blossom water (*mazaher*), 37,
    39, 125, 179

oranges, 2, 30, 31, 36, 157
    Orange Blossom Syrup, 5, 7–8,
        37–39, 106, 108, 109, 110,
        179
    Orange Dreamsicle, 142–43
    Orange Mascarpone, 5–6, 7–8
    Pan-Roasted Fresh Figs with
        Infused Honey Syrup and
        Orange Mascarpone,
        7–8
    zesting and juicing of, 7–8

P

panna cotta, Strawberry Panna
    Cotta, 93

Pan-Roasted Fresh Figs with Infused
    Honey Syrup and Orange Mas-
    carpone, 7–8

parfaits, 90, 173

Pasquette (little Easter), 87

Pastiera Napoletana (Nonni Maria's
    Ricotta Wheat Easter Pies),
    118–21

pastries, xvii, 23, 95, 170
    Apollo brand #7 phyllo pastry
        sheets, 37–39
    Basic Pastry-Double Crust/Lat-
        tice Top, 19–21, 177
    Basic Pastry-Single Crust, 9–10,
        176
    Chocolate Pastry, 28–29
    Cream Cheese Pastry, 31–32
    Figs in Baskets, 11–13, 49
    Rustica Pastry, 5, 11, 33–35, 120,
        178
    Shortbread Pastry, 94

Paterson, N.J., 3

Peace Offerings, 125

peaches, 161
    Fuzzy Navel (Peach Tiramisu),
        157–59

peach schnapps, 157

peanut butter
    Hound Dogs, 72–73
    Nutter Butter Finger Cakewiches,
        70–71
    Nutty at Heart, 82
    Peanut Butter Buttercream,
        66–67, 70, 72–73, 82, 185
    Peanut Butter Cakes, 68–69, 70
    in winter, 70–73

peanut butter and jelly (PB&J)
    PB&J Baby Bundts, 68–69
    PB&J Wonder Cakewiches, 66–67
    Wakile's childhood and, 65
    in winter, 64–69

pecan pies, xv, 51

pecans, 16, 27
    Itty Bitty Pecan Pies, 30–32, 49
    Pecan Filling, 31–32
    Pumpkin Ginger Pecan Sticky
        Buns, 45, 49

Petite Apple Pies, xvi, 15, 19–21

Petite Pumpkin Pies with Toasted
    Marshmallow Topping, 40,
    46–48

Phoenicia foods, 119

phyllo
    Knafeh Nests, 105–8, 109, 110,
        125
    Pignoli *Baklawa* Bites, 36–39, 49,
        125

picnics, 87

Pierri, Anna, 149–50

Pierri, Anthony, Jr., xiv, xvi, 51, 53,
    83, 87

Pierri, Anthony, Sr., 4, 53, 83, 92,
    105, 110, 127, 129, 131, 139,
    149–50

Pierri, Joseph, xiv, xvi, 51, 53

Pierri, Maria Domenica Gorga, xiv–
    xv, 4, 41, 51, 53, 72, 75, 83,
    127, 129, 139, 149
    la crema and, 89–92, 94

Pierri, Ralph, xiv, xvi, 51, 53, 83

Pierri, Regina, 92

Pierri, Rosie, xiv–xvii, 1, 41, 51, 53,
    75, 129, 139, 149

pies, xv, 51, 97
    Itty Bitty Pecan Pies, 30–32, 49
    Nonni Maria's Ricotta Wheat
        Easter Pies (*Pastiera Napole-
        tana*), 118–21
    Petite Apple Pies, xvi, 15, 19–21
    Petite Pumpkin Pies with Toasted
        Marshmallow Topping, 40,
        46–48

pignolis (pine nuts), 51, 56
    Blueberry-Pine Nut Filling, 109
    Blue Jays' Nests, 105, 109, 125
    Pignoli *Baklawa* Bites, 36–39, 49,
        125
    Pignoli Filling, 37–38

pineapples
    Beach Baby Blondies, 49, 112,
        114–15
    Pineapple Kabobs with Coco-
        nut-Key Lime Cream and
        Dulce de Leche Dunk,
        160, 164–66

Pink Lady, 134–35

pistachios, 2, 7, 9, 37
    Cardinals' Nests, 105, 110, 125
    Cherry-Pistachio Filling, 110
    Pistachio-Apricot Mezzelune,
        33–35, 49

pizzelles, 141
    Cinnamon Pizzelle, 167, 169
    Grilled Banana S'mores, 167–69

pizzettes
    Fresh Fig Pizzette Bar, 2, 5–6
    Pizzette Rounds, 2, 167

plums, Grilled Plums with
    Basil-White Balsamic Syrup
    and Lemony Crème Fraîche,
    161–63

pomegranates, 110

portion sizes, xvii, 37, 51

Presley, Elvis, 72

profiteroles, 97

puddings, 90–91

Lebanese Wheat Berry Pudding
    (*Sneyniyeh* or *Burbara*), 119,
    122–23

puff shells (choux), 96–102
    Chocolate Hazelnut Kisses, 101
    Pulcinelli Limoni (Little Lemon
        Chicks), 98–99
    Strawberry Shortcake Puffs, 100

Pulcinelli Limoni (Little Lemon
    Chicks), 98–99

pumpkins, xv
    canned purée and, 41–43
    carving of, 41
    in fall, 1, 40–48
    Petite Pumpkin Pies with Toasted
        Marshmallow Topping, 40,
        46–48
    Pumpkin Ginger Pecan Sticky
        Buns, 45, 49
    Pumpkin Spice Baby Bundts, 44
    Pumpkin Spice Babycakes, 42–45
    Wakile's childhood and, 41

Q

quick fixes, 173

R

ramekins, 16–17

raspberries, 26, 36
    Chocolate Volcanoes, 80–81
    Raspberry Drizzle, 55, 68–69,
        81, 182

ravioli, Caramel Apple Ravioli, xvi,
    15, 22–25

Real Housewives of New Jersey, The, xiii–
    xiv, 15, 33, 139, 193

Red Twizzlers, 75

Reese's, 75

rescue remedies, xvii

rice flour, 81

ricotta, 53
    Apple Ricotta Zeppolini, xvi,
        15, 18
    Nonni Maria's Ricotta Wheat
        Easter Pies (*Pastiera*

Napoletana), 118–21
ripples, Tangerine-White Chocolate
  Ripple, 78–79
rolls, Pignoli *Baklawa* Bites, 36–39,
  49, 125
Rome, 133, 144
Rosa, Aunt, xiv, 90
rosemary, Grilled Cherry-Rosemary
  Galettini, 170–72
rum, 102
rum raisin ice cream, 16
Rustica Pastry, 5, 11, 33–35, 120,
  178

S

Saint James church, 75
Sala Consilina, 90
salads, 4
salami, 65
Salerno, 90
salt, 169
  Sea-salted Caramel Drizzle,
    28–29, 180
  Tanned and Salty, 146–47
sandwiches, 64–65
  Hot Dogs, 73
  ice-cream, 141
sangria, Bottla Red, 136–37
sausage, 4
Seaside Heights, N.J., 142
shells, 13, 45, 90, 94–95
  see also puff shells
Shortbread Pastry, 94
shortcakes, Strawberry Shortcake
  Puffs, 100
Simple Syrup, 179, 181
s'mores, Grilled Banana S'mores,
  167–69
snacks, 33
Sneyniyeh (Lebanese Wheat Berry
  Pudding), 119, 122–23
spices, 33
  Pumpkin Spice Baby Bundts, 44
  Pumpkin Spice Babycakes, 42–45
spring, 87–123

birds' nests in, 104–10
blondies in, 112–15
brownies in, 112, 116–17
cream puffs in, 96–102
la crema in, 87–95, 97
Easter pies in, 118–21
Lebanese Wheat Berry Pudding
  (*Sneyniyeh* of *Burbara*) in, 119,
  122–23
sprinkle cookies, 51
star anise, 108, 133
Starburst, 75
Stella D'oro Swiss Fudge cookies, 94
sticky buns, Pumpkin Ginger Pecan
  Sticky Buns, 45, 49
stirring, xvii
strawberries, 2, 52, 161
  Strawberries-and-Cream,
    140–41
  Strawberry Panna Cotta, 93
  Strawberry Shortcake Puffs, 100
  Strawberry Topping, 93
streusels, 83
  Blueberry Streusel Baby Bundts,
    49, 84–85
struffoli, 51
sugar, 149, 169, 173
  Cinnamon Sugar, 18
sugar cookies, 51
summer, 1, 3–4, 127–72
  gelato in, 138–47
  granita in, 128–37, 139
  grilled desserts in, 160–72
  harvesting figs in, 3
  in New Jersey, xvi, 127, 131, 142,
    144, 146, 157
  tiramisu in, 148–59
Sunday Sauce, 4
Superstorm Sandy, 142
sweet potatoes, 46
swirls
  Caramel Swirl, 146–47
  Chocolate-Cherry Swirl, 144–45
syrups, 9
  Basil-White Balsamic Syrup,

    162–63
  Blue Jays' Nests, 105, 109, 125
  Cardinals' Nests, 105, 110, 125
  Doves' Nests, 105, 108, 125
  Grilled Plums with Basil-White
    Balsamic Syrup and Lemony
    Crème Fraîche,
    161–63
  Infused Honey Syrup, 5–6, 7–8
  Knafeh Nests, 105–8, 109, 110,
    125
  Maple-Brown Butter Glaze, 44
  Orange Blossom Syrup, 5, 7–8,
    37–39, 106, 108, 109, 110,
    179
  Pan-Roasted Fresh Figs with
    Infused Honey Syrup and
    Orange Mascarpone, 7–8
  Simple Syrup, 179, 181

T

tangerines
  Chocolate-Tangerine Baby
    Bundts, 76, 78–79
  Tangerine-White Chocolate
    Drizzle, 78–79
  Tangerine-White Chocolate
    Ripple, 78–79
Tanned and Salty, 146–47
tartlet pans, xvi
tarts, tartlets, 51
  Caramel Chocolate Walnut Tart-
    lettini, 26, 28–29, 49
  Chocolate Custard Tartlets,
    94–95, 125
  Figs in Baskets, 11–13, 49
  Grilled Cherry-Rosemary
    Galettini, 170–72
  Itty Bitty Pecan Pies, 30–32, 49
  Petite Apple Pies, xvi, 15, 19–21
Thanksgiving, xv–xvi, 46
Tia Maria, 151, 153
tiramisu, 51
  Capri Mia (Limoncello Tiramisu),
    xv, xvi, 155–57

tiramisu (continued)
  Cioccolato (Chocolate Tiramisu),
    xv, 125, 148, 153–54
  Fuzzy Navel (Peach Tiramisu),
    157–59
  in summer, 148–59
  Tradizionale (Classic Tiramisu), 49,
    151–52
  Wakile's childhood and, 149
Tony's Lemon Ice, 128–29, 131
toppings, 5, 54–55, 56–57, 58–59
  Almond Topping, 60–62
  Chocolate Hazelnut Cream,
    76–77
  Crumble Toppings, 16
  Marshmallow Cream, 40, 46–48,
    72–73, 167, 186
  Petite Pumpkin Pies with Toasted
    Marshmallow Topping, 40,
    46–48
  Strawberry Topping, 93
  Trader Vic's Kona, 151
  Tradizionale (Classic Tiramisu), 49,
    151–52
truffles, 101, 144

V

Valentine's Day, 82
vanilla ice cream, 8, 16, 161
vanilla pudding, 90

veal Milanese, 4
vegetables, 4
vinegar
  Basil-White Balsamic Syrup,
    162–63
  Grilled Plums with Basil-White
    Balsamic Syrup and Lemony
    Crème Fraîche, 161–63
Vino e Visciole, 144

W

Wakile, Joseph, Jr., xiii, xv, 23, 41,
  51, 63, 71, 87, 143
Wakile, Joseph, Sr., 4, 105, 110
Wakile, Kathy
  adolescence of, 53, 127, 139, 146
  baking enjoyed by, xiii–xiv
  childhood of, xiv, xvi, 1, 3–4, 27,
    41, 51, 61, 65, 75, 83, 87,
    89–90, 127, 129, 149
  creativity of, xiv, xvi, 89
  engagement of, 4
  heritage of, xiv–xv, 1, 3–4, 41,
    87, 90, 92, 112, 119, 139,
    149–50
  philosophy of, xvii
  physical appearance of, 112, 117
  sweet tooth of, xiii, 51, 75, 83, 97
Wakile, Rich, xiii, xv, 1, 4, 37, 51,
  71, 83, 103, 105, 124, 143

Wakile, Teta, xv, 4, 37, 105, 119
Wakile, Victoria, xiii, xv, 41, 51, 63,
  71, 110, 143
walnuts, 2, 27, 37, 58
  Bitsy Brunettes, 49, 112, 116
  Caramel Chocolate Walnut Tart-
    lettini, 26, 28–29, 49
  Chocolate Walnut Filling, 28–29
watermelon, 161
wheat berries
  Nonni Maria's Ricotta Wheat
    Easter Pies (*Pastiera Napole-
    tana*), 118–21
  Teta Melake's Lebanese Wheat
    Berry Pudding (*Sneyniyeh* or
    Burbara), 119, 122–23
whipped cream, 100, 133, 173
wine, 5, 144, 149, 153, 170
winter, 51–85, 87
  cheesecakes in, 51–62
  chocolate in, 74–82
  coffeecakes in, 83–85
  PB&J in, 64–69
  peanut butter in, 70–73
Wonder bread, 65
Wonder Cake, 66–67

Z

zabaglione, 149
  Cioccolato (Chocolate Tiramisu),
    xv, 125, 148, 153–54
zeppolis, zeppolinis, 87
  Apple Ricotta Zeppolini, xvi,
    15, 18
Zia Regina's Flan, xvi, 88, 92